# R O C K
# 'N' ROLL
# LONDON

# ROCK 'N' ROLL LONDON

## A GUIDE TO THE CITY'S MUSICAL HERITAGE

Tony Barrell

ACC ART BOOKS

arquee

# INTRODUCTION

Many towns and cities in the United Kingdom have contributed to the world's musical heritage. Run your finger over a map and you're bound to find the origin of an important singer or band. Sheffield has given us the Human League, Pulp and Arctic Monkeys. Glasgow has supplied Alex Harvey, Texas and Franz Ferdinand. Mick Jagger and Keith Richards came from Dartford, Kate Bush emerged in Bexleyheath, and Manic Street Preachers formed in Blackwood, Caerphilly.

But London has long been the hub of British music. Even before the sound of rock 'n' roll first blasted into the ears of British teenagers, this was the happening place, the big magnet for anyone with an ounce of musical talent and a scintilla of ambition. London has historically boasted the greatest concentration of record companies and recording studios, and the most legendary selection of live venues. Even when Merseyside had established its own lucrative brand of pop, the Beatles knew they had to up sticks and come down to London to make the most of their brilliance and to enjoy their fame to the full.

London has been the backdrop to many of the greatest moments and most notorious shenanigans of modern music. Take a trip around the city, hop off a bus or Tube and take a walk down a pavement somewhere, and it's very likely you'll be following in the footsteps of musical royalty through the rich heritage of rock 'n' roll. Some of the sites scream out at you – the David Bowie mural in Brixton, the zebra crossing clogged with tourists in Abbey Road, St John's Wood – but dozens of them are unrecognisable, anonymous and plaqueless. That restaurant you just passed in Chinatown was where Led Zeppelin had their very first ear-smacking rehearsal. That ordinary commercial premises in Piccadilly has a basement where Roxy Music recorded their otherworldly debut album. And that lovely old pub in North London is where Taylor Swift came all the way from America to shoot one of her videos.

So that's where this book comes in. Take it with you when you go wandering around the capital, and you'll quickly be able to locate and pay homage to the important places that played a part in rock 'n' roll history. It's very easy to get lost in this sprawling city, but with the *Rock 'n' Roll London* guide in your hand, you can get thoroughly lost in music instead.

For simplicity's sake, we have divided London into five basic areas: Central, North, West, East and South. The distinct Northeastern or West-Southwestern qualities of certain neighbourhoods have been put aside for our purposes. Also, several genres of music are represented in the book, but we're using the term 'rock 'n' roll' in its modern, overarching sense to include all the popular music of this century and the latter half of the 20th century. We're not arguing for a moment that, say, Roxy Music, Bob Marley and Goldfrapp can all be shoehorned into the narrow category of music exemplified by Bill Haley and His Comets.

*Tony Barrell, London*

# LIFE AND DEATH

Dozens of famous singers and musicians have lived in London – in Central and North London, for the most part. Many have been born here, some have squatted here, others have journeyed here from foreign lands, and the richest of the rich have bought mind-blowing mansions and stunning apartments here. That's why, if you spend some time wandering round the capital, you stand a good chance of spotting one or two familiar faces. Sadly, a growing number of rock 'n' rollers have died here – but many of the landmarks associated with them remain, and there are shrines and other places of pilgrimage where you can pay your respects. Here is a selection of notable residences and memorials.

Amy Winehouse, before the release of her debut album, *Frank*, in 2003. *Photograph Charles Moriarty*

# CENTRAL LONDON

## CLIFF RICHARD AND THE SHADOWS
**100 Marylebone High Street, W1**

Cliff and two members of the Shadows, guitarists Hank Marvin and Bruce Welch, were living in a humble flat here in 1959 when they had a musical epiphany: they took delivery of the first Fender Stratocaster guitar to be imported into England. Marvin was the first known English player of the iconic American model launched in 1954, and the bright red Strat, with its tremolo arm for heavenly vibrato effects, became his signature instrument – sparking a craze for electric guitars that has never died.

## THE BEATLES
**57 Green Street, W1**

The Fab Four stayed together in hotels when they came to London. But it presented problems for the hotels, which were continually besieged by screaming girls. So in late 1963, while they were recording their second album, *With the Beatles*, their manager Brian Epstein rented a flat in Mayfair where they could supposedly live peacefully together. Flat L on the fourth floor of 57 Green Street became the only home that the foursome ever shared – though this top-secret domestic arrangement only lasted a number of weeks, because Beatlemaniacs quickly sussed their whereabouts and became a nuisance.

## THE BEATLES
### 57 Wimpole Street, W1

In November 1963, not long after Paul McCartney began a relationship with Jane Asher, he left the group's communal pad in Green Street and went to live with the actress and her family here in Marylebone until early 1966. John Lennon was a frequent visitor, and many Beatles songs were worked on in the Ashers' music room in the basement, including 'I Want To Hold Your Hand', 'And I Love Her' and 'Eleanor Rigby'. Not all of this music was conceived while McCartney was conscious: one day, he awoke here after dreaming most of the melody to 'Yesterday'.

## PINK FLOYD
### 2 Earlham Street, WC2

In 1966, Pink Floyd's original singer, guitarist and chief songwriter, Syd Barrett, moved in to a top-floor flat in a row of run-down houses near the Marquess of Granby pub, off Shaftesbury Avenue in Covent Garden. Here he would take LSD, tinker with the I-Ching and, most importantly, experience a prolific burst of creativity, writing most of the songs that would appear on the band's debut album, *The Piper at the Gates of Dawn*. By the following year, Barrett had become withdrawn and his behaviour increasingly unpredictable, and his place in the band was eventually taken by David Gilmour. After a short solo career, Barrett became rock music's most famous and tragic recluse, living in his birthplace, Cambridge, until his death in 2006. He was the subject of the Floyd's 1975 anthem 'Shine on You Crazy Diamond'. The original row of houses in Earlham Street has long been demolished and replaced by unremarkable new buildings.

## DUSTY SPRINGFIELD
### 38 Aubrey Walk, W8

One of the greatest singers ever to emerge from Britain lived in this three-storey house in Notting Hill between 1968 and 1972, during which time she recorded classic songs including 'Son of a Preacher Man', 'Breakfast in Bed' and 'How Can I Be Sure'. The house contained a huge dressing room with an extensive wardrobe of glitzy dresses. But often, especially if Dusty had been drinking, the floors would be littered with domestic debris. She loved to smash crockery and throw food, and friends would cower in terror as the panda-eyed performer lobbed dinner plates and gateaux around with gay abandon.

## THE BEATLES/ JIMI HENDRIX
### 34 Montagu Square, W1

This outwardly respectable apartment in Marylebone has one of the most colourful histories to be found among London's rock 'n' roll properties. Ringo Starr leased the ground-floor-and-basement flat before his marriage to Maureen Cox in 1965, but they lived here for just a month or so before decamping to Surrey. In 1966 he rented the flat to his bandmate Paul McCartney, who set up a small studio in the basement to make avant-garde recordings for the Beatles' short-lived Zapple label. McCartney also began developing the song 'Eleanor Rigby' here. When the Zapple project failed to take off, McCartney moved out. In late 1966 it was rented to Jimi Hendrix, his manager Chas Chandler and their girlfriends. Hendrix wrote 'The Wind Cries Mary' here after a ferocious row with his girlfriend Kathy Etchingham. Starr evicted Hendrix and company a few months later, after they redecorated without permission (one story suggests they whitewashed the interiors, and another claims they painted them black). And in July 1968, when John Lennon needed a new base after leaving his wife Cynthia, he and Yoko Ono moved in here. This is where they were photographed for their notorious nude cover to the album *Unfinished Music No 1: Two Virgins*. In October the couple were the target of a heavy-handed police drug bust here, organised by the notorious Detective Sergeant Pilcher.

## THE BEATLES
**24 Chapel Street, SW1**

The Beatles' manager Brian Epstein based himself here in Belgravia, just west of Buckingham Palace, in the mid-1960s. In May 1967 the *Sgt Pepper's Lonely Hearts Club Band* album had its official launch at the house, leading Paul McCartney to meet his future wife Linda for the second time (Epstein's assistant Peter Brown was a friend and had chosen her as one of the official press photographers). In August of that year, Brian Epstein died here after an overdose of sleeping pills and alcohol. An inquest concluded that the death was accidental, though commentators have noted that he may have felt increasingly redundant since the Beatles had ceased touring and devoted themselves solely to recording. John, Paul, George and Ringo received the devastating news in Wales, where they were meditating with the Maharishi.

## JIMI HENDRIX
**23 Brook Street, W1**

Hendrix moved in to an upstairs flat here in Mayfair with his girlfriend Kathy Etchingham in 1968. They paid £30 a week in rent to the proprietor of the Mr Love restaurant downstairs, and shopped for textiles and antiques to make the apartment feel like home. The guitarist was intrigued to discover that George Frideric Handel had lived and died in the flat next door in the 18th century, and bought symphonies by the German composer on vinyl to listen to (the groovy shop One Stop Records was conveniently close by, in South Molton Street, and he was also known to frequent the HMV record store on Oxford Street). One day Hendrix reported glimpsing a bewigged man in the bathroom of the flat, which he took to be Handel's ghost. Hendrix lived here for much of the remainder of his life, which ended in 1970 at the Samarkand Hotel (see page 16). In 2016 the two adjoining Brook Street flats, numbers 23 and 25, opened as the museum Handel & Hendrix in London, which includes meticulous recreations of the rooms where the two very different music-makers lived.

Jimi Hendrix near the flat in Montagu Square that he rented from Ringo Starr.
*David Magnus/REX/Shutterstock*

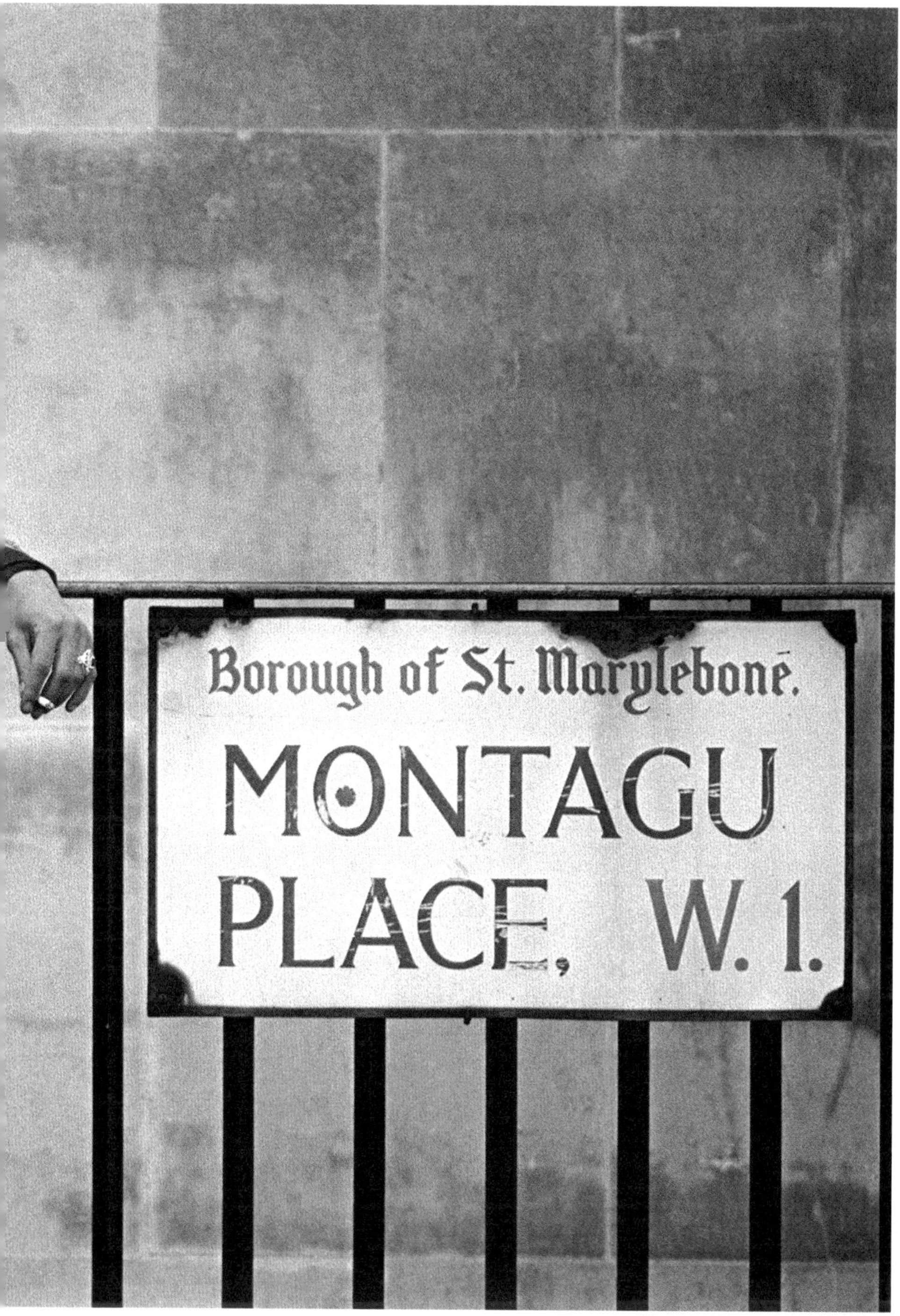
Borough of St. Marylebone.
MONTAGU
PLACE, W. 1.

# THE ROLLING STONES

**48 Cheyne Walk, SW3**

Mick Jagger bought this grand house in Chelsea in 1967 (when his bandmate Keith Richards was living at No. 3 in the same road), and his girlfriend Marianne Faithfull initially lived with him here. Jagger had his own studio built in the garden, where he wrote 'You Can't Always Get What You Want'. The song name-checks the Chelsea Drugstore, which was still at 49 King's Road back then – a hip superstore on three floors where you could buy the latest records, clothes and magazines. He also wrote 'Sympathy for the Devil' in Cheyne Walk, inspired by the novel *The Master and Margarita* by Mikhail Bulgakov, which Faithfull had been reading.

Not long after Jagger and Faithfull split up in 1970, he married Bianca Pérez-Mora Macías, who subsequently lived with him here. But when Jagger began an affair with the Texan model Jerry Hall in the late 1970s, Bianca filed for divorce and took out a court order forbidding him to enter the house until the annulment was finalised in 1980. Jagger and Hall later lived together at Downe House in Richmond-upon-Thames, until they split up and the Rolling Stone moved out.

# JIMI HENDRIX

**Samarkand Hotel,
21-22 Lansdowne Crescent,
W11**

The guitarist was hotel-based towards the end of his short life. He checked in to the Cumberland Hotel in Great Cumberland Place, Marylebone, on 6 September, 1970, where he gave his last-ever interview to the journalist Keith Altham. The Cumberland was his last official address. However, he died while spending time with his girlfriend Monika Dannemann at the Samarkand here in Notting Hill, a small residential hotel named after the ancient city in Uzbekistan. Early in the morning of Friday, 18 September, Hendrix returned to Lansdowne Crescent from a party, having consumed a great deal of alcohol, and reportedly took a large dose of sleeping tablets. An ambulance rushed him to St Mary Abbot's Hospital in Marloes Road, Kensington, where he was pronounced dead. His final official live performance had been 12 days before at the Open Air Love and Peace Concert on the German island of Fehmarn. The Samarkand Hotel has since closed, and the hospital has been demolished.

# LED ZEPPELIN
## Tower House, 29 Melbury Road, W14

The guitar god Jimmy Page bought this spooky 19th-century house in Kensington from the hellraising actor Richard Harris in 1972. Page paid £350,000 for the property, outbidding David Bowie. The architect of the Grade I listed building was William Burges, a leading light of the Victorian Gothic Revival, who went over the top with a series of elaborate decorative interiors, which include stained glass, ceramic tiles, painted murals, bespoke furniture and some of the weirdest fireplaces ever built. Page's next-door neighbour for many years was the film director and restaurant critic Michael Winner, for whom Page wrote the music for *Death Wish II*. In 2013, not long after Winner's death, his house (No. 31) was purchased by Robbie Williams, and almost immediately there was conflict between Williams and Page about the Take That star's plans for No. 31, which included proposals for basement excavation to build a subterranean swimming pool and gymnasium. Page wrote to the local council arguing that this major building work could have a 'catastrophic' impact on the fabric of his house. 'Having protected the Tower House for over 40 years,' he said, 'I am now continuing the fight against a new threat to this precious and unique building.'

# THE SEX PISTOLS
## 6 Denmark Street, WC2

The Greek bookshop known as Zeno was the place to come if you wanted to read about the wildlife of Mykonos or the history of the bouzouki. But in the mid-1970s, this shop on London's Tin Pan Alley hid a noisy secret. Behind

Graffiti by the Sex Pistols, still in situ at 6 Denmark Street (aka Tin Pan Alley).
*Photograph courtesy of Ian Martindale Photography*

it was a humble outbuilding in which Johnny Rotten and his bandmates could often be found rehearsing, before the Sex Pistols were launched on the world. They also had rough living quarters above the shop. Original Pistol Glen Matlock later recalled that Denmark Street gave the band 'somewhere to live away from our parents, a first real taste of independence. And it meant we had a regular rehearsal space – which we used nearly every day.' Their rehearsals could be interrupted by a doorbell outside – except that the mechanism was wired to a light instead of a bell, which they wouldn't have heard over their raucous playing. In the early 1980s, a few years after the Pistols moved out, the same address became home to Keren Woodward and Sara Dallin, two-thirds of Bananarama.

## MAMA CASS
**9 Curzon Place, W1**

Cass Elliot, the famously portly singer from The Mamas and The Papas, came to London in 1974 to play a series of sellout concerts at the London Palladium. The singer Harry Nilsson had suggested she save money on hotels and stay at his third-floor Mayfair flat, which he wasn't using at the time. Cass returned here after the final show, apparently relaxed and happy, and was discovered dead the next day, at the age of 32. A legend cruelly claims that she choked on a ham sandwich (a ham sandwich was found on her bedside table, but it was untouched). However, it is believed that her heart had been weakened by crash dieting.

## ROXY MUSIC
**82 Ladbroke Road, W11**

Bryan Ferry was living in this robust Victorian semi-detached house in Holland Park in 1975 when Roxy Music recorded their fifth album, *Siren*. The Texan model Jerry Hall was photographed for the cover, and she moved in here with the Roxy honcho as their romance blossomed. But in 1977 Hall left him for Mick Jagger, and Ferry sold the house for £80,000 to John Cleese. Fellow Python Michael

Palin paid a visit shortly afterwards, writing in his diary: 'We called round at his still-scaffolded Ladbroke Road house, recently acquired from Bryan Ferry, the singer and generally chic society figure. Huge rooms, and lots of them, and only John there, wandering through it, rather lost.' Cleese sold the house for £5 million in 2001.

## BOB MARLEY
### 42 Oakley Street, SW3

After arriving in London from Jamaica in the early 1970s, Marley and members of the Wailers had lived in cramped conditions in Bayswater and even Neasden. But in 1977, when they returned to the city for extensive recording sessions at Basing Street Studios (see page 152), the reggae star and his bandmates settled in a well-appointed flat in Oakley Street, Chelsea, between the King's Road and the River Thames. The band's cook, Gillie, prepared meals at the flat in accordance with the Rastafarians' strict Ital diet, including ackee, salt cod, dumplings and Irish moss, and whiffs of ganja perfumed the Chelsea air. A short trip across Albert Bridge took Bob Marley and his friends to Battersea Park, where they enjoyed casual football matches. David Bowie had lived in the same street, at No. 89, in 1974.

## THE WHO
### 9 Curzon Place, W1

In 1978, four years after Mama Cass had died here, The Who's drummer Keith Moon was using the same Mayfair apartment. On the evening of 6 September, he left the flat to attend a party and a screening of the film *The Buddy Holly Story*. He chatted with showbiz friends, including Paul and Linda McCartney, and was later said to be upbeat, if a little subdued – there were no major pranks or destructive larks from 'Moon the Loon' that night. After returning to Curzon Place, he took repeated doses of Heminevrin, which he had been prescribed to counter the symptoms of alcohol withdrawal. The next day his Swedish girlfriend, Annette Walter-Lax, found him lifeless. Like Mama Cass,

Bob Marley playing football in Battersea Park; The Wailers vs Island Records.
© *Bob Marley Music Ltd./Adrian Boot*

Keith Moon had survived to the age of 32. Owing to redevelopment, the address of the flat has since changed from 9 Curzon Place to 1 Curzon Square.

# MARVIN GAYE
**Park West Place, W2**

After a European tour in 1980, the Prince of Soul settled in London for a while. Life in the USA had became complicated: his divorce from his second wife was in progress, and the authorities were hounding him for unpaid taxes. His final address in the capital was a luxury Bayswater apartment near Marble Arch, loaned to him by a Nigerian businessman. While in London, Gaye resumed work on his 16th studio album, *In Our Lifetime*, recording mostly at the nearby Odyssey Studios in Castlereagh Street. In early 1981 he resumed his European wanderings and left England for Belgium.

# QUEEN
**Garden Lodge,**
**1 Logan Place, W8**

Freddie Mercury moved in to this Kensington house in 1986, the year when Queen released their album *A Kind of Magic* and played their final tour. For decades, the property's long garden wall has served as a canvas for fans' devotional graffiti. Freddie died here in 1991, shocking millions of people who were unaware that he had been suffering from AIDS. He was cremated at Kensal Green Cemetery, London W10, and some aficionados have perpetuated the legend that his ashes were scattered or buried at Logan Place. But the flamboyant lead singer had actually wanted a grander finale. 'I'd like to be buried with all my treasures, just like the pharaohs', he once said. 'If I could afford it, I'd have a pyramid built in Kensington.' He could easily have afforded it, but perhaps the local planning department would have had something to say about it.

## BOY GEORGE
**Carburton Street, W1**

In the late 1970s and early '80s, before he briefly conquered the world with Culture Club, George O'Dowd lived here in Fitzrovia, in a crumbling four-storey Georgian house, south of Regent's Park, that had become a squat for a colourful set of creative young people. George was sharing a downstairs room with his fellow cross-dresser and would-be pop star Marilyn, and elsewhere in the building lived the milliner Stephen Jones and the designer Melissa Caplan. The basement was prone to flooding, and the occupants shared a roofless outside lavatory. Boy George's fortunes improved in 1982, when Culture Club were signed by Virgin Records and topped the singles chart with 'Do You Really Want to Hurt Me'. The old house is gone now, demolished to make way for nondescript offices.

## KIRSTY MacCOLL
**Soho Square, W1**

After Kirsty MacColl was killed by a powerboat while swimming in Cozumel, Mexico, on 18 December, 2000, a proposal was sent to Westminster Council for the singer-songwriter to have her own memorial bench in the verdant surroundings of Soho Square. This is almost a holy place for fans, because she sang about 'an empty bench' here in the song 'Soho Square' on her 1993 album *Titanic Days*. The bench was unveiled on 12 August, 2001, as pigeons flew and MacColl's music played. The bench can be found near the southernmost edge of the square, near the northern ends of Frith Street and Greek Street. Devotees assemble here annually on the Sunday nearest her birthday, 10 October, to sing her songs and celebrate her life.

## MADONNA
**Great Cumberland Place, W1**

The Material Girl has been an avid buyer of bricks and mortar in London. In the early Noughties she paid an estimated £5 million for an eight-bedroom Georgian house in this Marylebone street, where she lived initially with her second husband, Guy Ritchie. She also bought some

Fan tributes to Freddie Mercury at the singer's former home at Logan Place, Kensington.
*Adnergje/creativecommons.org/licenses/by-sa/3.0/legalcode*

discreet mews cottages nearby. And in 2007, around the time she was recording her 11th studio album, *Hard Candy*, she paid another £6 million for the ten-bedroom house next door to her Great Cumberland Place abode, and had her own private fitness centre installed there. Property prices in Marylebone experienced a boom after Madge moved in, but her marriage collapsed and Ritchie moved out in 2008.

# KYLIE MINOGUE
## 53 Drayton Gardens, SW10

Kylie lived in a maisonette on the fifth and sixth floors of this mansion block in South Kensington for much of the Noughties, and had it expensively refurbished by the property developers Candy & Candy. The four-bedroom apartment had immaculate parquet flooring, an elegant staircase, and panoramic views over Chelsea. But evidently even that wasn't sufficiently opulent for the pint-sized pop princess, so she put the flat on the market in 2010 and shelled out £16 million for an apartment in the glitzy One Hyde Park development in Knightsbridge – another Candy & Candy production.

# ED SHEERAN
## Buckingham Palace, SW1

Born in Yorkshire and raised in Suffolk, Sheeran scraped an existence as a teenage drifter in London between 2008 and early 2011 as he tried to crack the music business. He would sometimes sleep on the Circle Line of the Underground, and he has recalled that he also spent 'a couple of nights' sleeping rough outside Buckingham Palace, after he discovered a nearby arch with a heating duct. Appropriately, he wrote his song 'Homeless' here. Life changed when his records began selling in huge numbers in 2011, and in December 2017 he returned to the Palace – to collect his MBE.

# THE CRANBERRIES

## Hilton Hotel, Park Lane, W1

Known for emotive songs such as 'Zombie', 'Linger' and 'Ode to My Family', Dolores O'Riordan of the Cranberries possessed one of the most haunting voices in rock 'n' roll. In early 2018 the 46-year-old Irish singer was in London for a recording session and staying at this five-star hotel in Mayfair. On Monday, 15 January, hotel staff found her dead in her room. An inquest found that she had drowned in the bath in an accident caused by alcoholic intoxication.

# NORTH
# LONDON

## JOE MEEK
**304 Holloway Road, N7**

One of Britain's greatest recording pioneers lived and worked here, in a flat above a shop selling leather goods. Joe Meek produced some memorable hits of the pre-Beatles era, including 'Johnny Remember Me' by John Leyton (1961) and 'Have I the Right?' by the Honeycombs (1964). Meek was ahead of his time in his sonic experimentation and in his use of the recording studio as an instrument. His most famous legacy is the 1962 instrumental 'Telstar' by the Tornados, which he wrote and produced, and which not only topped the UK chart but was the first record by a British rock band to reach number one on the US Hot 100. Musicians who recorded in this Holloway Road studio include David Bowie, Billy Fury, Jimmy Page, Ritchie Blackmore, Tom Jones and Screaming Lord Sutch. Meek also occupied himself here by trying to commune with the spirit of Buddy Holly using a ouija board, and he risked his liberty before the decriminalisation of homosexuality by loitering in the streets to find gay lovers. His life ended tragically here on the eighth anniversary of Buddy Holly's death, 3 February, 1967, when a fiery row with his landlady, Violet Shenton, ended with him shooting her dead and then turning the gun on himself.

## THE KINKS
### 6 Denmark Terrace,
### Fortis Green Road, N10

Ray Davies and his younger brother Dave grew up here with their parents in the 1950s in this suburb of Muswell Hill, where they learned to play guitar and mastered skiffle and rock 'n' roll songs. The house was often the scene of lively musical parties and singalongs. The brothers attended the local William Grimshaw Secondary Modern School and formed the Ray Davies Quartet, which included Ray's classmate Pete Quaife, who would be recruited as bass player when the Kinks formed in the early 1960s. Dave Davies was caned and expelled from the school for failing to attend classes and having sex with a girl on the school grounds – an experience that inspired the song 'The Hard Way' on the Kinks' 1975 album *Schoolboys in Disgrace*.

## T. REX
### 25a Stoke Newington
### Common, N16

Born on 30 September, 1947, Mark Feld (later reborn as Marc Bolan) lived with his parents and elder brother Harry until 1962 at this three-storey house in a predominantly Jewish neighbourhood. His mother, Phyllis, sold fruit on a market stall in Soho, and his father, Simeon, was a lorry driver.

## THE BEATLES
### 7 Cavendish Avenue, NW8

Paul McCartney bought this detached three-storey house in St John's Wood for £40,000 in 1965, and it became his London base a year later after undergoing renovation. The Beatles would often meet here before going to record at EMI Studios in Abbey Road, which was just five minutes' walk away. Apple Scruffs (dedicated female Beatles fans) would sometimes linger for hours by the high wall and wooden gate that shielded the property from the road. After a small party of Scruffs used a ladder to gain access to the house, McCartney wrote the song 'She Came in Through the Bathroom Window'.

Ringo and Paul with his dog Martha at McCartney's home in Cavendish Avenue, St John's Wood.
*Photograph Tom Murray*

## ROD STEWART
**507 Archway Road, N6**

Roderick David Stewart was born in this house in Highgate to an English mother and Scottish father in the final year of World War II. Young Rod played with toy trains here and became an energetic footballer. Like Ray and Dave Davies of the Kinks, he attended William Grimshaw Secondary Modern School in Muswell Hill. Seized by a passion for rock 'n' roll, 'Rod the Mod' spent the 1960s dressing up and singing hoarsely in a succession of largely forgotten bands, before finally hitting the big time with 'Maggie May' and the album *Every Picture Tells a Story* in 1971 (see page 143).

## THE ROLLING STONES
**10a Holly Hill, NW3**

After Mick Jagger and Keith Richards moved in to a flat here in Hampstead in 1965, their songwriting partnership found a new gear. The Stones' career had been launched with cover versions – songs by artists including Chuck Berry, Buddy Holly, and even Lennon/McCartney ('I Wanna Be Your Man'). But their shrewd manager Andrew Loog Oldham knew that the big money was in self-penned songs. At their previous flat (33 Mapesbury Road, Brondesbury), Oldham had urged them to write together, and had even locked them indoors one evening, insisting that they compose a song before his return. However, for months, forgettable tunes like 'Shang a Doo Lang' and 'That Girl Belongs to Yesterday' were all they could produce. Finally, in the more spacious and upmarket apartment at Holly Hill, they turned out their number-one classic 'The Last Time' – which began a run of Jagger/Richards hits and paved the way for one of the longest-surviving bands of all time.

## ELTON JOHN
**29 Furlong Road, N7**

Elton John was living in a basement flat near Highbury & Islington Tube station with the lyricist Bernie Taupin in 1968. They had just established their unorthodox method of songwriting, which began with a rough set of Taupin lyrics for Elton to write music to, but they had yet to find success.

Elton's then fiancée Linda Woodrow moved in with them here, but the singer agonised over the impending wedding. Linda had no interest or belief in his music, and there was also the small matter of Elton's sexuality. At one point, Taupin found him with his head in the oven, apparently trying to commit suicide, though the lyricist saw it more as a cry for help: 'He'd only turned the gas on to "low" and he'd left the kitchen window open. And he'd even thought to take a cushion to rest his head on too.' The blues singer Long John Baldry, chosen as best man, talked Elton into reconsidering his future and the wedding was cancelled. The episode was set to music seven years later as the hit song 'Someone Saved My Life Tonight'.

## BRIAN ENO
### 49 Leith Mansions, Grantully Road, W9

Eno moved into this ground-floor two-bedroom apartment in Maida Vale during his synthesizer-twiddling days in Roxy Music, and it became a hive of musical experimentation after he left the band in 1973. The cover of his debut solo album, *Here Comes the Warm Jets*, shows part of the interior cluttered with an arty assortment of objects. Eno retreated to this flat to recuperate in January 1975, after he was knocked down by a taxi following a recording session in Notting Hill. His friend Judy Nylon came to visit and put an album of harp music on his barely functioning stereo. And as Eno lay there, half-listening to occasional notes mingling with the pitter-patter of the rain outside, he was inspired to begin creating what he called 'ambient music'. By the time he finally sold the flat in 1994, he was a highly esteemed record producer, having contributed to David Bowie's Berlin Trilogy as well as throwing sonic fairy dust over albums by U2, Talking Heads, Ultravox and other assorted artists.

## BANANARAMA
### 5, 7 & 9 Malden Place, NW5

When Bananarama first appeared on *Top of the Pops*, they were still on the dole, and were wearing hoods at the DHSS office to conceal their newfound fame. But by 1984, old friends Keren Woodward, Sara Dallin and Siobhan Fahey had enough money to splash out on three neighbouring houses in this out-of-the-way street in Kentish Town. It was the way pop groups were supposed to live, as popularised by the Beatles in the movie *Help!* (though the girls didn't go so far as creating one huge Bananaramic interior). The domestic idyll lasted until 1987, when Fahey married Dave Stewart and quit the band shortly afterwards.

## OASIS
### 9 Steeles Road, NW3

Noel Gallagher bought this five-storey Victorian house in Belsize Park in 1996, the year after Oasis released their chart-busting second album, *(What's the Story) Morning Glory?* The guitarist had a fanlight installed above the front door to declare its name as Supernova Heights, after his song 'Champagne Supernova', the album's closing track. The house quickly became notorious for its raucous late-night parties, such as the bash for Noel's 30th birthday in May 1997, when Sex Pistols songs were played at deafening volume and the police came knocking. In 1999 Noel and his then wife, Meg Mathews, sold the house and moved out to the country. In 2005 it was bought by the comedian David Walliams, who made extensive renovations and then put it back on the market in June 2018.

## LILY ALLEN
### 92 Brondesbury Road, NW6

Lily Allen was living here in Kilburn in 2009 when she topped the album and singles charts with *It's Not Me, It's You* and 'The Fear', respectively. It was in this road, near Queen's Park Tube station, that she was repeatedly harassed by paparazzi – on one occasion a photographer even crashed into her car – and she obtained a High Court injunction to prevent camera-wielding nuisances from pursuing her or coming within 100 metres of her home.

# AMY WINEHOUSE
## 30 Camden Square, NW1

The brilliant but troubled chanteuse bought this robust Victorian house in a relatively quiet part of Camden in 2010. The Grammy-winning singer had a strong emotional connection with this bohemian London borough: she had performed many times at the Dublin Castle pub, and was a regular at the Hawley Arms pub near Camden Market. On 20 July, 2011, Amy Winehouse appeared on stage at the nearby Roundhouse, singing with her goddaughter Dionne Bromfield as part of the iTunes Festival. It would be her final public performance. Three days later, on the afternoon of Saturday, 23 July, she died in her home from alcohol poisoning. Soon after the news broke, an area opposite the house became an evolving shrine, with fans leaving flowers, notes, vodka bottles, wineglasses and beer cans. The house was sold a year later for £1.9 million, but the tributes have continued to be left outside.

# GEORGE MICHAEL
## 5 The Grove, N6

The former Wham! singer bought this swanky property within easy reach of Hampstead Heath for more than £7 million in 2002, and set up a sophisticated home recording studio here. Some of the Highgate locals were equally starry: for a while his neighbour at No. 6 was Annie Lennox, until she sold her house to the actor Jude Law in 2005. Sting and his wife Trudi Styler were also nearby, having bought No. 2 The Grove from the violinist Yehudi Menuhin in 1995. Towards the end of his life, George Michael reportedly enjoyed late-night parties with friends at this house. After he died on Christmas Day, 2016, at his country house in Goring-on-Thames, Oxfordshire, fans created an informal 'memorial garden' outside his Highgate home. The star was buried near his mother's grave in nearby Highgate Cemetery.

# ADELE
## Shelbourne Road, N17

Adele Laurie Blue Adkins grew up in a small flat on this road in Tottenham, near the incongruous wildlife haven of Tottenham Marshes. Born on 5 May, 1988, the singer was brought up by her unmarried mother, Penny Adkins, after her father, Mark Evans, left the family home when she was a baby. Adele lived here for the first nine years of her life, during which time she absorbed a wide range of music – including 'Lovesong' by the Cure, which she later covered on her second album, *21*. She and her mother left London in the 1990s to live in Brighton, but the young girl disliked her new surroundings in the Sussex seaside town. 'The people seemed really pretentious and posh,' she later complained, 'and there were no black people there. I was used to being the only white kid in my class in Tottenham.' In 1999, Penny and her daughter moved back to London, and seven years later Adele signed a recording contract and was well on the way to stardom and a shelfful of Grammys.

Fan tributes to Amy Winehouse, Camden Square, 2011. *Dutourdumonde Photography/Shutterstock.com*

# W E S T
# L O N D O N

## THE POLICE
**11 Gunterstone Road, W14**

In the Swinging Sixties, more than a decade before he joined the Police, the guitarist Andy Summers lived in one of several flats occupied by hip young musicians here in West Kensington. 'We were a sort of commune, I suppose,' he once recalled. 'I was living basically in one tiny room. I had a guitar and about 700 LPs stacked along one wall, including a lot of esoteric music that I was interested in – African, Indian and Balinese music – and I had a collection of books on Zen.' This was the building where Summers had his first taste of LSD. And shortly after he arrived in Britain in 1966, Jimi Hendrix called at this house to borrow a guitar. Andy Summers left the house and moved to West Dulwich in 1968, when he was asked to join the band Soft Machine.

## RONNIE WOOD / PETE TOWNSHEND
**The Wick, Richmond Hill, TW10**

This detached Georgian house in leafy Richmond-upon-Thames, with magnificent views over the Thames, has links with the Rolling Stones, The Who, the Faces and David Bowie. In 1972, Ronnie Wood, then the guitarist in the Faces, bought the house from the veteran actor John Mills. Wood had a studio rigged up in the basement, and an especially starry session in 1973 produced the first recording of 'It's Only Rock 'n' Roll', which subsequently became a hit for the Stones. The original tape featured Wood on guitar, Kenney Jones of the Faces on drums, and both Mick Jagger and David Bowie on vocals. Keith Richards once camped out for several months in a house in Wood's garden, to avoid the police attention he was receiving at his own home in Chelsea. Ronnie Wood eventually became an official member of the Stones in 1976. He left the Wick 20 years later, when Pete Townshend of The Who bought the house for £2 million.

## T. REX
**Queens Ride, SW15**

On 15 September, 1977, Marc Bolan and his girlfriend Gloria Jones enjoyed an evening out at Morton's Club in Mayfair. Gloria was driving them home early the next morning in a purple Mini 1275GT when she lost control of the car here in Barnes, and crashed into a fence post and a sycamore tree. Gloria was injured, but Marc died instantly. He was less than a mile from his home, at 142 Upper Richmond Road West in East Sheen, and two weeks shy of his 30th birthday.

The crash site, on Queens Ride near the junction with Gipsy Lane, became a makeshift shrine when grieving fans attached flowers, messages and photographs to the tree. In 1999 the T. Rex Action Group was granted ownership of the land, and a more elaborate memorial has since been created. A bronze bust of the glam-rock star now stands here, engraved with lines from his song 'Child Star':

## QUEEN
**22 Gladstone Avenue, TW14**

Seventeen-year-old Farrokh Bulsara and his parents settled in this small pebble-dashed house in Feltham, just a few miles from Heathrow Airport, after leaving their home country of Zanzibar in 1964 when their lives were threatened by a bloody revolution. Farrokh studied art at Isleworth Polytechnic and Ealing Art College, though his overwhelming passion was music. In the early 1970s he changed his name to Freddie Mercury and teamed up with Brian May, Roger Taylor and John Deacon to form Queen and bring a kind of magic to the world of rock 'n' roll.

## THIN LIZZY
**184 Kew Road, TW9**

Shortly after the release of Thin Lizzy's successful live double album *Live and Dangerous* in 1978, the band's frontman and bass player Phil Lynott bought this imposing five-bedroom house in Richmond, on the corner of Kew Road and Fitzwilliam Avenue, opposite the Lion's Gate entrance to Kew Gardens. The charismatic rocker lived here with Caroline Crowther (daughter of comedian Leslie Crowther), whom he married in 1980. Lynott put a jukebox in his study and converted the garage into a basic recording studio. He remained here after the band split up in 1983, but soon fell prey to his addictions to heroin and alcohol. On Christmas Day 1985 he collapsed in the house, and was eventually taken to Salisbury Infirmary and diagnosed with septicaemia. He died on 4 January, 1986, at the age of 36.

## THE CLASH
**101 Walterton Road, W9**

The number of this house in Maida Hill was used to name a pub-rock band, the 101ers, most of whose members were using the place as a squat around 1974. They included the vocalist Joe Strummer, then in his early twenties, who would find fame a few years later in the Clash. Strummer and some of his friends had a second squat nearby at 23 Chippenham Road. The 101ers played original material alongside rock 'n' roll and R&B covers, and in April 1976 they were booked at the Nashville club in Earl's Court, where they were supported by a little-known punk band called the Sex Pistols. Strummer was stunned from the moment he heard the Pistols that night. 'Five seconds into their first song and I knew we were like yesterday's papers,' he later recalled. 'I mean, we were over.'

# LONDON'S LOST MAGAZINES

The music papers, style sheets and fanzines that mattered, and where they were based

INTERNATIONAL TIMES, Originally based at 6 Mason's Yard, SW1, it later moved to 102 Southampton Row, WC1: Magazine for intelligent hippies of the late-'60s counterculture.

NEW MUSICAL EXPRESS (NME), 23 Denmark Street, WC2; 15-17 Long Acre, WC2; 128 Long Acre, WC2; King's Reach Tower, Stamford Street, SE1; 5-7 Carnaby Street, W1: Essential reading for discerning rock fans, especially in the '70s.

MELODY MAKER, 19 Denmark Street, WC2; 161-166 Fleet Street, EC4; 168-173 High Holborn, WC1; King's Reach Tower, Stamford Street, SE1; 24-34 Meymott Street: The serious weekly for musicians and fans of jazz, soul and folk.

OZ, 70 Clarendon Road, W11; 40 Anhalt Road, SW11; 38a Palace Gardens Terrace, W8; 52 Princedale Road, W11; 19 Great Newport Street, WC2; 39 Goodge Street, W1: Psychedelic, satirical and scandalous monthly, first published in Australia, which may hold a record for its different London addresses.

NOVA, Tower House, Southampton Street, WC2: Radical, intelligent and stunningly designed glossy for women.

STREET LIFE, Brownlow House, 50-51 High Holborn, WC1: Short-lived but brilliant left-wing '70s music fortnightly, which published long articles on drugs, abortion and contract killers.

SNIFFIN' GLUE, 24 Rochfort House, Grove Street, Deptford, SE8: Passionate punk fanzine written by young bank clerk, Mark Perry, on a children's typewriter in South London.

SMASH HITS, Mappin House, 4 Winsley Street, W1: Young people's music magazine, brimming with wit and style.

THE FACE, 5 Mortimer Street, W1; Exmouth House, Pine Street, EC1: Hip '80s monthly style bible with its own Neville Brody-designed typeface.

BLITZ, 1 Lower James Street, W1; 40-44 Newman Street, W1: Eclectic and readable rival to The Face.

# E A S T
# L O N D O N

## THE SMALL FACES
### 308 Strone Road, E12

The singer Steve Marriott grew up in a flat in this Victorian house in Manor Park, after being born prematurely at East Ham Memorial Hospital on 30 January, 1947. His mother, Kay, was a factory worker and his father, Bill, had a local fish stall where he sold shellfish as well as that great cockney staple, jellied eels. Bill was also a pub pianist, and he bought young Steve a ukulele, which the boy quickly mastered. Steve soon graduated to full-sized guitars, and by 1965 had teamed with Ronnie Lane, Kenney Jones and Jimmy Winston (later replaced by Ian McLagan) to create the Small Faces and bring mod style and psychedelic music to the masses.

## KATE BUSH
### Wuthering Heights, 99 Court Road, SE9

This huge six-bedroom house in Eltham was a tranquil London hideaway for Kate Bush between 1985 and 2003, during the period when she worked on albums such as *The Sensual World* and *The Red Shoes* and then temporarily retreated from the music industry. An amusing story claims that at some point in her 12-year gap between albums, she invited executives from her record company, EMI, to sample her 'latest work' here. When they arrived, breathlessly expecting to hear some new music, they were shown a batch of cakes she had just baked. A subsequent owner of the property installed some gates emblazoned with the name

'Wuthering Heights'. Although this was the official name of the house during Bush's tenure (referencing her chart-topping debut single of 1978), the singer would never have advertised it so clearly – she values her privacy much too highly.

## DAMON ALBARN
### 21 Fillebrook Road, E11

Born in 1968, the Blur frontman and Gorillaz co-founder was raised in Leytonstone, in this robust-looking house near Epping Forest. His father was an artist and furniture designer and his mother was a theatrical set designer, and Albarn has described his former home as a 'pretty zany house'. Though it appeared ordinary from the outside, it had silver-painted interiors, 'and there were mad kind of plastic bright-coloured blocks, which were our furniture'. He referenced his Leytonstone upbringing on his 2014 solo album, *Everyday Robots*, and paid a return visit to the area before the record's release – surprising the locals at the Red Lion pub with a spontaneous rendition of 'Parklife'.

## DIZZEE RASCAL
### Bow Cross estate, E3

The grime star grew up on the Crossways estate, built in the 1970s and dominated by three 25-storey tower blocks, referred to locally as 'the Three Flats'. Once actually known by some as 'the Pride of Bow', the Crossways estate became a depressing watchword for social deprivation, neglect, addiction and crime. But it was also the 1990s seedbed for Dizzie Rascal's innovative brand of urban music, as expressed in his Mercury Music Prize-winning 2003 debut album, *Boy in da Corner*. Crossways was later the object of a regeneration programme, losing its sinister concrete walkways and gaining green communal spaces along with a new name: Bow Cross. Dizzee has enjoyed a series of platinum-selling albums and number one dance hits, and his appeal stretches far beyond his East London origins: the actor Brad Pitt once revealed that he used the star's song 'Bonkers' as exercise music.

# "THIS PLACE BUILT ME, MAN. SO MUCH LEGACY HERE AND CREATIVITY HERE"

DIZZEE RASCAL

Crossways estate, Bow; childhood home of Dizzee Rascal.
*Suttonpubcrawl/creativecommons.org/licenses/by-sa/3.0/legalcode*

# SOUTH LONDON

## DAVID BOWIE
**40 Stansfield Road, SW9**

Bowie was born David Robert Jones in this three-storey Victorian house in Brixton on Wednesday, 8 January, 1947 – the 12th birthday of the as-yet-unknown Elvis Presley. David's parents, Haywood 'John' and Margaret 'Peggy' Jones (née Burns), had recently met in Tunbridge Wells. The Jones family would live here until 1953, when they relocated to the more salubrious town of Bromley, in Peggy's home county of Kent.

## IAN DURY
**40 Oval Mansions, SE11**

The singer lived in a flat here in Kennington with his teenage girlfriend Denise around 1974, when he was in his early thirties and fronting the pub-rock band Kilburn and the High Roads. Dury called the place 'Catshit Mansions'. The flat was poky, though it offered interesting views: the Oval cricket ground on one side, and Kennington gasworks on the other. Fame arrived after the singer signed to Stiff Records in 1977 and released the single 'Sex & Drugs & Rock & Roll', which had been co-written in this flat by Dury and his musical collaborator Chaz Jankel.

## BON SCOTT
**67 Overhill Road, SE22**

Bon Scott, remembered as one of the greatest frontmen in rock, was lead singer of the Australian band AC/DC from 1974. One night in February 1980, after attending the Music Machine club in Camden Town, the 33-year-old star was left to sleep in a friend's Renault 5 parked in this East Dulwich road. He was later found unresponsive and rushed to hospital, where he was pronounced dead. Speculation has long surrounded the cause: while the death certificate blames 'acute alcohol poisoning', it has also been suggested that he had overdosed on heroin or suffered an asthma attack. AC/DC discussed disbanding after the tragedy, but decided to continue, recruiting the singer Brian Johnson. Their subsequent album, the highly successful *Back in Black*, was a tribute to Bon Scott, whose grave in Fremantle, Australia, is one of the country's most visited sites.

## PULP
**Sceaux Gardens, SE5**

The singer Jarvis Cocker lived in a block of council flats on this Peckham estate in the early 1990s, when he was on the brink of fame. Around the same time, he was studying fine art and film at Central Saint Martin's College on Charing Cross Road – later immortalised in the Pulp classic 'Common People'.

## DAVID BOWIE
**Tunstall Road, SW9**

This famous mural, inspired by Bowie's lightning-streaked depiction on his 1973 album *Aladdin Sane*, was painted in 2013 by the Australian street artist James Cochran as part of the art exhibition *The Many Faces of Bowie*. It adorns Morleys department store in Tunstall Road, Brixton, south of Bowie's birthplace in Stansfield Road. Less than three years after its creation, the mural became a magnet for hordes of fans stunned by the news of the star's death on 10 January, 2016, two days after his 69th birthday and the release of his album *Blackstar*.

James Cochran's mural of David Bowie, close to the singer's birthplace in Brixton.
*Photograph Fatima Luna/iStock*

# MEETINGS AND HAPPENINGS

To fully appreciate the lives of the rock 'n' roll stars, we have to venture out from their birthplaces and homes to the locations where they found inspiration, attracted attention and had life-changing moments. This chapter celebrates the chance encounters that created famous bands, the things that rock 'n' rollers have done in their spare time, and some of the strangest things that have happened to musicians in London.

Led Zeppelin in 1969: (L-R) Jimmy Page, John Paul Jones, Robert Plant, John Bonham. *Adc/REX/Shutterstock*

# CENTRAL LONDON

## CLIFF RICHARD AND THE SHADOWS
**The Swiss Tavern,**
**53 Old Compton Street, W1**

For his earliest forays in showbiz, Cliff Richard was known by his original name, Harry Webb. By 1958 he was attracting attention as the singer in a band called the Drifters. The group were asked to play a ballroom in Derbyshire, but the venue's manager, Harry Greatorex, was insistent on one condition: they should follow the fashion of the times and have the lead singer incorporated in their name, like Frankie Lymon and the Teenagers. The trouble was, 'Harry Webb and the Drifters' didn't sound terribly rock 'n' roll. A meeting took place over drinks at this Soho bar, then known as the Swiss Tavern, which was attended by Greatorex, Harry Webb, his manager John Foster, and assorted Drifters. The name 'Cliff' was tossed around, and Foster suggested 'Cliff Richards'. The guitarist Ian Samwell amended that to 'Cliff Richard', saying that it would be a boon for publicity: most people would say 'Richards' and when they were corrected, they would have heard the name twice. Cliff's debut single, 'Move It' – often hailed as the first British rock 'n' roll disc – shot to No. 2 later that year.

## PINK FLOYD
**University of Westminster,**
**309 Regent Street, W1**

Three members of Pink Floyd – bassist Roger Waters, keyboardist Rick Wright and drummer Nick Mason – met at this college in the early 1960s, when it was known as Regent

Street Polytechnic. They were supposed to be studying architecture, but it was a very liberal establishment: Waters was allowed by one laid-back lecturer to sit in the corner and play guitar during lessons. In early 1963 the three formed a band with a changing cast of other members, but they couldn't settle on a name, calling themselves Sigma 6, the Tea Set and the Screaming Abdabs, among other things. At one point they were Megadeaths (predating Megadeth by two decades). The classic early Floyd line up was eventually completed by the Camberwell-educated guitarist and singer Syd Barrett, who borrowed the names of two American bluesmen, Pink Anderson and Floyd Council, to coin their most enduring name. One of the Floyd's live bootlegs is appropriately called *Music for Architectural Students*.

## DAVID BOWIE / T.REX

**Dick James Music,
132 Charing Cross Road, WC2**

In the summer of 1964, David Bowie and Marc Bolan were two as-yet-unsuccessful teenage musicians who shared the same manager, Les Conn. They finally met when they were both summoned one day to Conn's office here, at Dick James Music on the corner of Denmark Street. Disappointingly, Conn didn't require them for their musical abilities that day: he wanted them to roll up their sleeves and paint his office. Still known back then by their real names, David Jones and Mark Feld, the two flashily dressed singers quickly became friends, despite the fact that Bolan (as Bowie later recalled) rudely declared Bowie's shoes to be 'crap'. But when Conn came back from lunch, he found the pair had downed their brushes and skedaddled without finishing the job.

## JIMI HENDRIX

**Freddy Bienstock,
17 Savile Row, W1**

The Beatles weren't the first musical invaders to penetrate the snooty, fine-tailoring sanctum of Savile Row. For most of the 1960s, No. 17 was the headquarters of Freddy Bienstock, who published songs recorded by Elvis Presley,

# "ONLY BY TRYING ON OTHER PEOPLE'S CLOTHES DO WE FIND WHAT SIZE WE ARE."

JOHN LENNON

Cliff Richard and many other acts. This roomy Georgian building also had rehearsal space for hire, and in October 1966, shortly after his arrival in Britain, Jimi Hendrix came here to try out drummers for his new power trio. The guitarist and his bass-playing colleague Noel Redding jammed at high volume with a series of hopefuls and ended up with a shortlist of two men: Mitch Mitchell and Aynsley Dunbar. Hendrix flipped a coin, Mitchell won, and the lineup of the Jimi Hendrix Experience was complete.

## THE BEATLES
**Raymond Revue Bar,
11 Walker's Court, W1**

On 18 September, 1967, the Beatles visited the notorious Raymond Revue Bar to film a sequence for their madcap film *Magical Mystery Tour*. They sat rather sheepishly in the audience as the professional stripper Jan Carson disrobed to the music of the Bonzo Dog Doo-Dah Band, who played 'Death Cab for Cutie'. Exactly 500 days later, the Beatles would be involved in another controversial London performance: their legendary bash on the rooftop in Savile Row.

## THE BEATLES
**Apple Boutique,
94 Baker Street, W1**

The Fab Four briefly became clothing merchants when they opened the Apple Boutique here in December 1967, on the corner of Paddington Street. Its hippyish fashions were designed by the Dutch art collective known as The Fool, who also decorated the exterior with a huge psychedelic mural, which had to be painted over when the proprietors of local businesses complained. In July 1968 the band decided to concentrate on their music rather than selling threads, and spontaneously gave away thousands of pounds' worth of shirts, dresses, jackets, trousers, jewellery and furniture to a huge crowd of lucky shoppers.

The Beatles watching topless dancer Jan Carson at Raymond Revue Bar, 1967.
*Keystone/REX/Shutterstock*

## YES

**La Chasse club,
100 Wardour Street, W1**

The prog-rock band Yes has had a bewildering number of incarnations, with keyboard players and other virtuosos continually packing their bags and being replaced by new faces. On more than one occasion, there have been two different versions of the group operating at the same time. But the long-abiding foundation of the band was created by singer Jon Anderson and bassist Chris Squire, who met here in May 1968 at an upstairs club called La Chasse, along the road from the Marquee club. During that encounter, they found they had a common passion for the music of the Beatles and Simon & Garfunkel. Anderson went on to sing in Squire's colourfully named band Mabel Greer's Toyshop, and as various long-haired musos departed and joined, it evolved into Yes. The snappy new name came from the original guitarist, Peter Banks.

## LED ZEPPELIN

**39 Gerrard Street, W1**

In August 1968, a cramped basement in Soho reverberated to the earliest notes played by a promising new rock group. This is where guitarist Jimmy Page, singer Robert Plant, drummer John Bonham and bassist John Paul Jones assembled for their first rehearsal. The basement had been the original home of Ronnie Scott's jazz club, which had now moved to Frith Street. The quartet launched into the bluesy 'Train Kept A-Rollin' (originally recorded by the American musician Tiny Bradshaw in 1951), which Page had already played with his previous band, the Yardbirds, and it was evident that they gelled extraordinarily well. Page later remembered: 'As soon as we played together, everyone knew instinctively that we'd never played anything like that before. And it was just so right.' Originally known as the New Yardbirds, the group honed their bluesy hard rock on a tour of Scandinavia before returning to London to record their debut album and settle on a new name. They became Led Zeppelin – a phrase borrowed from Who drummer Keith Moon, who joked about bands going down like a gigantic lead balloon.

## MOTT THE HOOPLE
**Regent Sound Studios,**
**4 Denmark Street, WC2**

In 1969 a Hereford band called Silence, in need of a lead vocalist, were auditioning singer after singer at Regent Sound Studios and almost giving up hope. Along came another unpromising candidate: 30-year-old Ian Hunter from Shrewsbury, wearing sunglasses and looking overweight in his corduroy suit. But Hunter impressed the band's manager, Guy Stevens, with a performance of Bob Dylan's 'Like a Rolling Stone', and was provisionally accepted by the band. Stevens renamed the group Mott the Hoople, after a novel he had read in prison (he had previously given the band Procol Harum their name as well). Mott finally hit the jackpot in 1972 with 'All the Young Dudes', a song given to them by their famous admirer David Bowie, and went on to have two hit albums of mostly Hunter-penned songs – *Mott* (1973) and *The Hoople* (1974) – before Hunter left the band. Mott the Hoople's other fans have included Morrissey, Mick Jones of the Clash, and even Benazir Bhutto.

## THE TROGGS
**DJM Studios,**
**71-75 New Oxford Street,**
**WC1**

The Troggs had tasted success with Sixties songs such as 'Wild Thing' and 'With a Girl Like You', but their career was on the wane in 1970 when music publisher Dick James brought Reg Presley and his bandmates here, to DJM Studios, for a second bite of the cherry. They planned to record a number called 'Tranquillity', but it probably didn't help that these studios had a peculiar layout: there was no visual link between the control room and the recording areas. What actually ensued was a long verbal disagreement, which was captured on tape by a quick-thinking engineer, unbeknown to the band. Later circulated to guffaws among music-business people, the result is one of the funniest and most expletive-packed recordings ever made. *The Troggs Tapes* are said to contain no fewer than 137 swearwords, many of them beginning with 'F'. This audio gem became one of the inspirations behind both *Derek and Clive* and *This Is Spinal Tap*.

# GENESIS

## Old Barracks, Kensington Palace, W8

Late one night in 1971, something downright weird happened in these barracks, where the parents of Peter Gabriel's girlfriend Jill lived. The Genesis frontman was enjoying a profound philosophical conversation with Jill and the record producer John Anthony, when suddenly the windows blew in and the room became freezing cold and strangely smoky. Jill's face appeared to change and she began talking in an unfamiliar voice. Having seen plenty of horror films, Gabriel reacted by making a cross out of some household items, including a candlestick, whereupon Jill became violent and had to be restrained. At some point, Gabriel thought he saw spooky figures in white cloaks outside. The whole bizarre event (which wasn't generated by drugs, apparently) set him thinking about the battle between good and evil, inspiring many of the lyrics of 'Supper's Ready'. Clocking in at about 23 minutes on the band's 1972 album *Foxtrot*, the epic song is a widely acknowledged classic of progressive rock.

# LED ZEPPELIN

## Equinox bookshop, 4 Holland Street, W8

For much of the 1970s this small premises off Kensington High Street was an occult bookshop, Equinox, set up by none other than Led Zeppelin axemeister Jimmy Page. He started the business because he had found it frustratingly difficult (in the pre-internet age) to find the obscure books on the magic arts that he wanted to read. The shop was named after an epic work by the notorious Aleister Crowley, and it not only sold books but published them as well. Early releases were *The Book of the Goetia of Solomon the King*, translated by Crowley, and *Astrology: A Cosmic Science* by Isabel M. Hickey. But there may not have been enough weirdo customers to make the bookshop a success, and Led Zeppelin took up so much of Page's time that by 1979 the shop had ceased trading. Nonetheless, his interest in the occult remained; he was still talking about star signs in 2010, when he reflected on the astrological power of the band: 'Oh, it was quite interesting astrologically. Because you had Robert, a Leo, as a frontman, which is perfect... And you had two Capricorns – John Paul Jones and I – and then you had John Bonham, which is the twins, Gemini. Astrologically, I could see there was a sort of power, if you like, there.' Stripped of its spooky cobwebs and dark corners, the Equinox shop later became the premises of the celebrity photographer Richard Young.

## THE SEX PISTOLS
### Sex, 430 King's Road, SW10

This shop in the World's End area of the King's Road became a womb for the embryonic British punk-rock movement. Malcolm McLaren and Vivienne Westwood established themselves here in 1971, selling retro wear for rockers, bikers and teddy boys. In the early days, vintage rock 'n' roll blared from an old Wurlitzer jukebox in the shop. The business was called Let It Rock, then Too Fast To Live Too Young To Die, before settling on Sex and shifting its focus to fetish clothing, including bondage gear. Glen Matlock worked at the shop, Steve Jones and Paul Cook hung out here, and they auditioned Johnny Rotten on the premises and became the Sex Pistols. Before McLaren and Westwood moved in, this was Mr Freedom, a boutique for Sixties trendsetters.

## GARY NUMAN
### Piccadilly Circus
### Underground Station, W1

One day in 1975, when Gary Numan was a 17-year-old unknown called Gary Webb, he apparently saw a ghost on the London Underground. He and a friend walked off a Tube train onto a platform at Piccadilly Circus, and they were chatting about their ambitions for forming a band as they followed a crowd of passengers heading for the exits. Right in front of them, Numan saw the back of a man wearing a hat and a long grey coat. At the top of the escalator, Numan and his friend continued to trail the man, who walked into a passage to the left – and then the two teenagers were confronted with a solid wall. 'It looked as if the corridor we were in had been sealed countless years before', the star recalled years later. 'No sign of the man. We both checked with each other that we had been following the man, and then realised that all the other passengers had gone. We ran as fast as we could out of the station.' The spooky experience later inspired the artwork for Numan's albums *Dance* (1981) and *I, Assassin* (1982).

## DAVID BOWIE / KATE BUSH
**The Dance Centre, 12 Floral Street, WC2**

Bowie studied movement and dance with the legendary Lindsay Kemp at the Dance Centre here in Covent Garden in the late 1960s. The singer later said of Kemp: 'His day-to-day life was the most theatrical thing I had ever seen, ever. It was everything I thought bohemia probably was.' Kate Bush, who would also be inspired by Kemp, came to the same place in the mid-1970s to learn dance with the tutor Robin Kovac, and to study with the American mime artist Adam Darius. The building later became the Sanctuary spa, and has since been converted into offices.

## THE POLICE
**26 Green Street, W1**

The drummer Stewart Copeland was living in a swanky apartment here in Mayfair in January 1977 when Gordon 'Sting' Sumner arrived in London and looked him up, having previously met him in Newcastle upon Tyne. The American tub-thumper and the Geordie bassist began rehearsing in the spacious flat with the Corsican guitarist Henri Padovani. The Police briefly became a quartet when guitarist Andy Summers joined. But then Padovani was dismissed, and the bleach-headed trio went on to conquer the world. The band's manager, Miles Copeland (father of Stewart), once worked for the CIA, and the neighbouring property, 27 Green Street, also has an espionage connection: it was the birthplace of James Bond writer Ian Fleming in 1908.

## THE ROLLING STONES

**Sticky Fingers restaurant,
1A Phillimore Gardens, W8**

Bill Wyman opened his restaurant Sticky Fingers here in 1989, around the same time that the 52-year-old bass player married his 19-year-old girlfriend Mandy Smith. The site, between Kensington High Street and Holland Park, was offered to the London restaurateurs Terry Mitchell and Claudio Obertelli, who knew that it had been home to a series of failing restaurants. But after they heard on the grapevine that Wyman fancied having his own eatery, the trio joined forces. Wyman named the restaurant after the Stones' 1971 album (rejecting the name Beggars Banquet) and put American favourites such as burgers and ribs on the menu. He had always been the great collector in the Stones, saving all manner of equipment and trivia relating to the band, and the nicotine-yellow-painted walls of Sticky Fingers became an opportunity to display some of his vast hoard of guitars, gold discs and posters. Generous amounts of insulation were installed in the ceiling as a barrier between the restaurant's sound system and the residents of the flats upstairs.

## MADONNA

**Punchbowl pub,
41 Farm Street, W1**

In March 2008, when the singer was still married to Guy Ritchie, they bought the Punchbowl public house near Berkeley Square in Mayfair for about £2.5 million. This was Madge's brief 'real-ale period', when she was telling all and sundry that she adored Timothy Taylor's Yorkshire-brewed bitter. The distinguished Grade II listed pub dates from Georgian times, when its saloon and public bar rang with the laughter and gossip of coachmen and grooms from Berkeley Mews. Ritchie took over his ex-wife's share of the boozer when the marriage failed later that year, and cashed it in five years later.

## LADY GAGA

**Heaven,**
**Under the Arches,**
**Villiers Street, WC2**

Revellers at the G-A-Y night at Heaven on 27 October, 2013, were stunned when a striking blonde woman in a white dress appeared unexpectedly on stage and began singing an unfamiliar song about the goddess of love and the planets of the solar system, which featured a pun on Uranus. The word went round, correctly, that this was Lady Gaga. The star was treating the crowd to her new single, 'Venus', but they didn't know that they had an even bigger treat in store. As the song came to an end, she stepped out of the dress and became completely naked.

## FLORENCE + THE MACHINE

**Liberty,**
**Great Marlborough Street, W1**

In June 2018, Liberty launched a limited-edition sleepwear range as a result of a collaboration between the department store and Florence Welch. The 31-year-old singer hand-picked a selection of floral prints from the vast Liberty archive to adorn pyjamas, kimonos, camisole-and-panties sets and eye masks. Welch, who has often sported kimonos on stage at Florence + The Machine gigs, confessed that she was 'a Liberty print obsessive' who often wore nightwear during the daylight hours: 'I do a lot of writing in the early morning, still in my pyjamas, with lots of very strong coffee.'

Lady Gaga performing at G-A-Y, Heaven, in October 2013. *REX/Shutterstock*

# NORTH LONDON

## THE BEATLES
**Decca Studios,
165 Broadhurst Gardens,
NW6**

Back in 1962, New Year's Day was an ordinary working day for most people. And that was the day when the Beatles travelled all the way by road from Liverpool to Decca Studios in West Hampstead to perform a test session, in the hope of securing a recording contract. They recorded 15 songs, including the early Lennon/McCartney compositions 'Hello Little Girl' and 'Love of the Loved', and covers of 'Till There Was You' and 'The Sheik of Araby'. But Decca decided to reject them, telling their manager Brian Epstein that 'Guitar groups are on the way out'.

## THE SEX PISTOLS
**306-316 Euston Road, NW1**

One of the most memorable TV interviews of all time may not have happened if Freddie Mercury hadn't gone to the dentist near the end of 1976. Queen were due to appear on Thames TV's *Today* programme on 1 December, but had to pull out owing to their frontman's dental complications. Filling the gap were the Sex Pistols, whose reputation as controversial punk rockers preceded them. Hapless 53-year-old presenter Bill Grundy asked whether the band's recent receipt of £40,000 from EMI might be 'slightly opposed to their anti-materialistic view of life', and was assured by bassist Glen Matlock that it wasn't. 'Well, tell me more, then,' he said. 'We've fuckin' spent it, ain't we?'

retorted guitarist Steve Jones. 'Really?' asked Grundy. 'Down the boozer,' elaborated Jones. When a faltering Grundy engaged in some light verbal flirting with one of the 'girls behind' – none other than Siouxsie Sioux – Jones called him a 'dirty sod' and a 'dirty old man'. 'Well, keep going, chief, keep going', said Grundy. 'Go on, you've got another five seconds – say something outrageous.' 'You dirty bastard!' said Jones. 'Go on, again', baited Grundy. 'You dirty fucker!' said Jones. 'What a clever boy', said Grundy sarcastically, wrapping up the interview and telling the band he hoped he'd never see them again. The Pistols danced to the show's closing theme music. As a result of the incident, the Pistols were banned from various concert venues around Britain, their single 'Anarchy in the U.K.' was hoicked off the BBC playlist, and within weeks they were ditched by EMI. Grundy was suspended for two weeks, and the *Today* show was axed altogether in early 1977. The building where the encounter had happened was demolished in the 1990s.

# MADNESS
**AH Holt,**
**5 Kentish Town Road, NW1**

People travelled from far and wide to this shop, AH Holt, to buy Dr. Martens boots when they were scarcer than they are now. It was a short walk from Camden Town Tube station and next door to the much-loved Rock On record shop, reinforcing the link between music and hip footwear. But the office space above the shoe shop was once even cooler, being directly involved in the 2 Tone ska revival. In 1979 this was the domain of Rick Rogers, who managed the Specials and Selecter, as well as the Damned. When Rogers moved to premises further along the road, the office at No. 5 was taken over by the band Madness, who released their first single on 2 Tone Records. Madness rehearsed here and shot parts of their videos in and around the building. The AH Holt shop later changed its name to the British Boot Company.

The Sex Pistols on the 1976 *Anarchy Tour*: (L-R) Glen Matlock, Johnny Rotten, Steve Jones and Paul Cook.
*Ray Stevenson/REX/Shutterstock*

## PRINCE
**New Power Generation,
21 Chalk Farm Road, NW1**

On 30 April, 1994 – shortly after topping the UK charts with the song 'The Most Beautiful Girl in the World' – Prince came to Camden personally to open his very own London shop. Fans queued for hours along the Chalk Farm Road for a chance to see him and buy Prince paraphernalia. He wasn't going by that name at the time, having changed his identity to an unpronounceable symbol, and the shop was called New Power Generation (the name of his backing band and one of the songs on his album *Graffiti Bridge*; the phrase had also appeared on his earlier album *Lovesexy*). Devotees paid homage as the Artist Formerly Known as Prince finally appeared on an upstairs balcony with his girlfriend Mayte Garcia and gave a two-fingered peace sign. For two years you could come to the NPG shop to buy all manner of purple items, including incense and symbol-decorated pencils, and watch videos of his performances in an upstairs café. But customers complained that there wasn't enough actual music on sale here, and the star appeared to lose interest in the shop, finally letting it go in 1996. He would have enjoyed the fact that the building later enjoyed a brief existence as a lingerie store.

## DIDO
**Café Flo,
334 Upper Street, N1**

As a young Londoner in the 1990s, Dido Florian Cloud de Bounevialle O'Malley Armstrong worked as an accident-prone waitress at the popular French eatery Café Flo in Islington. 'I was very clumsy, but my heart was in it,' Dido recalled years later. One day, wielding a magnetic window pole, she accidentally brought the main light fittings down, and they had to close the restaurant for two days. 'And then I dropped about 16 glasses over Stephen Fry, when I was carrying too many. He was remarkably pleasant about it – I wouldn't have been.'

## ELTON JOHN
**St Pancras Station, N1**

Rail passengers coming and going at this vast station did an aural double-take on 4 February, 2016: somebody was playing 'Tiny Dancer' (from the 1973 album *Goodbye Yellow Brick Road*) on a piano, and it sounded exceptionally good. It sounded like Elton John – and the gathering crowd confirmed that it was indeed Sir Elton himself. His album *Wonderful Crazy Night* was due out the next day, and the instrument he was playing was his own gift to the station. 'Surprise!!' the singer wrote on Instagram. 'I popped into St Pancras International to christen the Yamaha piano which I donated to the station. Now everyone can have a play.'

## STORMZY
**Postal Museum,**
**15-20 Phoenix Place, WC1**

One Saturday in September 2017, the grime star teamed up with Adidas and JD Sports to commandeer a double-decker bus and give 40 of his fans a two-hour tour of his home city. The journey began at the Brixton Academy, where he had recently played a series of sold-out gigs. The bus – emblazoned with with a giant portrait of the star, along with his name – continued northwards through south London, crossed Tower Bridge and eventually headed for the West End. The vehicle stopped near JD Sports in Oxford Street so that Stormzy could pick up some fresh Adidas trainers for the fans, and made its way finally to the Postal Museum in Clerkenwell, where Stormzy played a surprise gig to hundreds of cheering fans. 'I love my fans and love my city', he said, 'so I wanted to bring the two together.'

Prince exiting the New Power Generation shop in Camden Town, 1994.
*Tom Pilston/The Independent/REX/Shutterstock*

# W E S T
# L O N D O N

## THE ROLLING STONES/
## THE BEATLES
**Crawdaddy Club,**
**1 Kew Road, TW9**

Between 1962 and 1963 the Rolling Stones were attracting serious attention as the resident band at the Crawdaddy Club, based in the back room of the Station Hotel, opposite Richmond railway station. And on the evening of 14 April, 1963, came the historic first meeting between the two groups who would tower over Sixties pop. That day, the Beatles had recorded an appearance on the TV show *Thank Your Lucky Stars* at Teddington Studios (miming to the song 'From Me to You'), and afterwards they decided to drive to Richmond and see the Stones play. The Fab Four stood conspicuously in the audience, wearing long suede jackets and matching hats. They were impressed with their rivals' sound, and they gave the Stones front-row tickets and backstage passes for their own televised show four days later at the Royal Albert Hall.

## ROD STEWART
**Twickenham Station, TW1**

Roderick Stewart was discovered at the age of 19 when he was heard busking on a platform at Twickenham railway station in January 1964. He had just been to see the blues singer Long John Baldry at the famous Eel Pie Island. Stewart looked bizarre, wearing a number of scarves, but the sound he was making, as he sang and played Howlin' Wolf's 'Smokestack Lightning' on his harmonica, was good enough to attract the attention of Baldry on the opposite platform. Baldry crossed the bridge to Stewart's platform and asked him if he wanted to join his band, offering a pay packet of £35 a week. Stewart accepted, and the group, complete with 'Rod the Mod', soon enjoyed a weekly residency at the Marquee club. (Stewart is often credited with playing the harmonica solo on Millie Small's 1964 hit 'My Boy Lollipop', but he has denied the claims.)

## THE WHO
**Oldfield Hotel,**
**Oldfield Lane, UB6**

Back in 1964, Keith Moon was the drummer in a band called the Beachcombers. But in April he came to the Oldfield Hotel in Greenford to watch a gig by the Detours – an early incarnation of The Who – who often played here. Their previous drummer had left the band, and they were playing with a session drummer called Dave Golding. Moon asked the manager of the club to introduce him to the group, and then asked if he could play a couple of numbers with them on the drums. They consented in spite of his laughable appearance: he had dyed ginger hair and was wearing a ginger corduroy suit. The band, plus Moon, launched into the Bo Diddley song 'Road Runner', and Moon attacked the kit with gusto – the first thing he broke was the bass-drum pedal. Pete Townshend, Roger Daltrey and John Entwistle were impressed, and invited him to join the band shortly afterwards.

## QUEEN
**89 Goldhawk Road, W12**

Freddie Mercury obtained a cheap brand-new notebook from a shop here in Shepherd's Bush, in which he jotted down lyrics for many new Queen songs. The blue Challenge notebook came up for auction in 2016, and was snapped up by an anonymous buyer for £62,500. A small label on the front cover identifies it as coming from 89 Goldhawk Road. Freddie is likely to have bought the book in early 1988, when the band started recording their album *The Miracle*, because the shop was close to the studios – Townhouse, also in Goldhawk Road – and many of the lyrics in the book relate to tracks on that album (including 'Khashoggi's Ship', 'I Want It All' and the title track). He evidently continued to use the notebook when Queen moved on to their next album, *Innuendo*, because the book includes lyrics to 'These Are the Days of Our Lives', 'The Show Must Go On' and other tracks on that album (which was recorded elsewhere). The notebook also contains sketches by Mercury and written contributions from his bandmates.

## MICHAEL JACKSON / PULP
### Earls Court Exhibition Centre, SW5

The Brit Awards ceremony was held here in February 1996, and saw gongs going to Oasis (British Album of the Year), Björk (International Female Solo Artist) and Brian Eno (British Producer of the Year). But the most memorable event of the night was the moment when Jarvis Cocker of Pulp sabotaged a performance by Michael Jackson – winner of the Artist of a Generation award. Jackson cut a Christ-like figure on stage as he sang 'Earth Song', ending up in pure white clothing as he was surrounded by actors, many of them children, pretending to worship him. Finding the whole thing insufferably pompous, Cocker jumped up on stage, lifted his shirt and wiggled his bottom in Jackson's direction as 'a form of protest'. Jacko's next UK performance, at Wembley Stadium the following year, was his last one in this country.

## THE SPICE GIRLS
### 80 Wood Lane, W12

It's widely believed that the Spice Girls' catchy nicknames – Posh Spice, Ginger Spice, Baby Spice, Scary Spice and Sporty Spice – must have been a cynical marketing ploy by their management. In fact, the names emerged spontaneously here in Wood Lane, Shepherd's Bush, in the offices then used by the BBC's *Top of the Pops* magazine. Staff of the magazine enjoyed a promotional lunch with the girls in 1996, and then put together a feature on the new band. To illustrate it, some head-shots of the quintet were superimposed on a photograph of five kitchen spice jars. The editor of the magazine, Peter Loraine, decided that it would be fun to give them alternative names, and over the course of several minutes of brainstorming, the now-legendary handles were coined. 'I think Posh Spice was the first one,' recalled Loraine, 'the joke being that she so *wasn't* posh – she was from Essex – but she had a black Gucci dress on and pouted all the way through that lunch. Mel B became Scary Spice mainly because she had sat on my knee during the lunch; she was quite intimidating.' There were some rejections before they emerged with the final names for the feature. 'Ginger Spice was Saucy Spice at one point, and Mel C we were going to call Scouse Spice.'

## OASIS / THE BEATLES
**Westminster Register Office, 97-113 Marylebone Road, NW1**

Liam Gallagher was married twice at Westminster Register Office. In 1997 the Oasis singer was hitched here to his first wife, the actress Patsy Kensit; they split up three years later. And in 2008 the mercurial Mancunian rocked up here again to wed All Saints singer Nicole Appleton; they divorced in 2014. This building, previously known as Marylebone Register Office, has also seen three more successful Beatles weddings: that of Paul McCartney and Linda Eastman in 1969 (whose marriage lasted nearly 30 years until Linda's death in 1998), Ringo Starr and Barbara Bach in 1981, and McCartney and Nancy Shevell in 2011.

## PETE DOHERTY
**Bankrobber Gallery, 52 Lonsdale Road, W11**

The Libertines and Babyshambles singer displayed examples of his artwork in public here in May 2007. The month-long exhibition, at the Bankrobber Gallery in Notting Hill, included drawings to which 28-year-old Doherty had added his own blood. The collection was said to have been inspired by Doherty's troubled life, which has seen him repeatedly arrested for drug offences.

Javis Cocker, defiant after a post-Brit Awards court appearance, 1996. *Photoshot/Getty Images*

# EAST LONDON

## THE ROLLING STONES
**176-180 Romford Road, E15**

Driving home after playing a gig in Romford, Essex, on 18 March, 1965, the Stones found themselves in trouble after answering the call of nature. When bass player Bill Wyman announced that he needed to urinate, they pulled into a petrol station here in Forest Gate – Francis Motor Service Ltd – and Wyman approached the attendant and asked to use the facilities. As the attendant later recalled, 'a shaggy-haired monster wearing dark glasses alighted to enquire, "Where can we have a leak here?"' The outraged attendant replied that there was no lavatory they could use on the premises, whereupon Wyman retreated to the car – but promptly returned with bandmates Mick Jagger and Brian Jones to confront the man again. Still receiving no joy, Jagger said 'We'll piss anywhere, man,' and they unzipped and coated a nearby wall. Police were alerted, and a few months later the three miscreants were charged by a magistrate with 'insulting behaviour' and fined 15 guineas. Ironically, by this time they were topping the charts with '(I Can't Get No) Satisfaction'.

## DIRE STRAITS
**White Swan pub,**
**Greenwich High Road, SE10**

In the 1970s, before Dire Straits were formed, the guitarist and songwriter Mark Knopfler watched a band playing Dixieland jazz in the White Swan pub (often simply known as the Swan) on this site. The place was almost deserted, and he was struck by the pitiful quality of the ensemble. He later recounted: 'They're an interesting make-up, those kind of bands, in that they're blokes who do all sorts of things, aren't they? They're postmen, they're draughtsmen, whatever – quantity surveyors, teachers, different things...' Knopfler was amused when one of the band thanked the audience and announced that they were 'The Sultans of Swing', and the experience inspired Dire Straits' best-loved song. Other pubs have claimed the story for themselves, but in an interview in the band's heyday, Knopfler told the tale and clearly located it here, saying his brother David 'was living somewhere down in Greenwich and we just went out to the pub – I think it was called the Swan, something like that, in Greenwich High Road...' The pub has since been demolished, and an apartment block now stands here.

## MICHAEL JACKSON
### River Thames at Tower Bridge, E1

The King of Pop made his most grandiose and narcissistic visual statement while plugging his 1995 double album, *HIStory: Past, Present and Future, Book 1*. When Sony executives asked Jackson for ideas for promoting the work, he is said to have replied: 'Build a statue of me.' They went further and built nine 32ft-high effigies, depicting the 36-year-old singer in his favourite pseudo-military garb, and sent them to tower over selected sites in European cities. The London one was floated on a barge down the Thames on 16 June, the day before the album's release, and onlookers gawped as the two sections of Tower Bridge were raised to allow the steel-and-fibreglass colossus through. The statue was subsequently moored by the Tower of London for a week, frightening the ravens.

# LONDON'S LOST SHOPS

The boutiques and stores – gone but not forgotten –
where musicians and fans bought clothes, books and beautiful things

**GRANNY TAKES A TRIP, 488 King's Road, SW10:** Bright and groovy clothes for '60s swingers, often inspired by artefacts from olden times, such as William Morris floral prints.

**I WAS LORD KITCHENER'S VALET, 293 Portobello Road, W10:** Antique military clothing for rock stars and their imitators. The business started on a market stall before opening in Portobello Road, and then progressed to Foubert's Place (off Carnaby Street) and Piccadilly Circus. Hendrix was a customer.

**HUNG ON YOU, 22 Cale Street, SW3; 430 King's Road, SW10:** A mecca for '60s dandies. A 1966 magazine gushed that 'The Rolling Stones, faithful customers, are sensational in Hung On You's moss-coloured hipster pants, cream pongee jackets, flowered shirts, Byzantine ties and white leather cordovan boots'.

**GANDALF'S GARDEN, 1 Dartrey Terrace, SW10:** Hippie emporium in Chelsea that sold clothes, handmade pottery, health food, mystical objects and books about new-age subjects like astrology and reincarnation. For a short time it published a mind-blowing magazine of the same name.

**INDIACRAFT, 51 Oxford Street, W1:** 'The Treasure House of Indian Handicrafts', which sold everything from joss sticks to saris and tablas, was the shop in the West End where George Harrison bought his first sitar in 1965. (It had another branch at 254 Kensington High Street, W8.)

**MR FISH, 17 Clifford Street, W1:** Mayfair boutique that sold beautiful clothes made from rich fabrics such as silk, velvet and brocade. Jagger's androgynous Hyde Park stage outfit came from here, as did the dress Bowie wore on the cover of his 1970 album *The Man Who Sold the World*.

**PX, 57 Endell Street, WC2:** Basically a big dressing-up box for New Romantics in the 1980s. If you wanted a frilly shirt, a Robin Hood jacket or a pirate belt, you came to Covent Garden. (The first PX shop was round the corner in James Street.)

**ELVISLY YOURS, 233 Baker Street, NW1:** An emporium devoted to the King of Rock 'n' Roll. If you couldn't find a particular Elvis item here, it probably didn't exist. The shop left the building in 2010, but the business moved online.

**HELTER SKELTER, 4 Denmark Street, WC2:** Much-missed shop specialising in books about music, which traded from 1995 to 2004. Its stock of Bob Dylan books and fanzines was particularly comprehensive. The shop was on the site formerly occupied by Regent Sound Studios, where the Stones cut their first album, and the cash desk stood where the studio's mixing desk had been.

## MARC ALMOND
**Cannon Street/New Change, EC4**

The former Soft Cell singer had a brush with death while riding pillion on a motorcycle on Sunday, 17 October, 2004. Almond was thrown from the saddle in a collision with a car at this junction near St Paul's Cathedral, and suffered serious head injuries. The 48-year-old singer was described as being in critical condition, but over the next few weeks he made a miraculous recovery in hospital. Several years later, he admitted that he had passed the site of the crash and imagined his life ending there. 'I sometimes drive past the spot where it happened, and I see myself lying in the road,' he said. 'I lived round the corner from Freddie Mercury when he died, and people created this shrine of poems and flowers and teddy bears, and I've sometimes wondered if my fans would've done the same for me.'

## KYLIE MINOGUE
**Old Blue Last pub,
38 Great Eastern Street, EC2**

On Thursday, 13 February, 2014, Kylie Minogue fans were enjoying a Kylie-themed evening at the curvaceous Old Blue Last pub in Shoreditch, singing karaoke versions of her hits as well as playing 'Kylie bingo'. The petite Australian songstress wasn't scheduled to appear in person. But suddenly a familiar figure bounded onto the stage. Wearing a skimpy black outfit and accompanied by barely dressed female dancers, 45-year-old Minogue sang material from her latest album, *Kiss Me Once*. One of the songs, 'Into the Blue', seemed to name-check the old pub itself, while the raunchy dance moves may have referenced the fact that it was once a brothel.

# SOUTH LONDON

## THE BONZO DOG DOO-DAH BAND
**162c Rosendale Road, SE21**

The 1960s' strangest and funniest band was formed in September 1962, when the art students Viv Stanshall and Rodney Slater met at this flat in West Dulwich, near Brockwell Park. Slater was already in an informal trad-jazz combo, and Stanshall joined the band to transform it with his own brand of eccentricity and mayhem. The name of the new band came from mixing up words at random, using a Dadaist cut-up technique not dissimilar to the method David Bowie later used to write lyrics (Bonzo Dog was a reference to a British cartoon character from the 1920s). The group would alternate between innovative musical comedy ('The Intro and the Outro') and relatively straightforward pop ('Urban Spaceman').

## CREAM
**154 Braemar Avenue, NW10**

In the summer of 1966, the living room of Ginger Baker's ground-floor maisonette in Neasden became the scene of the first rehearsal by the supergroup comprising Baker on drums, Eric Clapton on guitar, and Jack Bruce on bass and vocals. Bruce had initially voiced misgivings about the project (Baker had threatened him with a knife when they had played together in the Graham Bond Organisation), but the three musicians were immediately thrilled with the sound they made together here. Deciding they were the *crème de la crème* of the British music scene, Clapton coined the name 'the Cream' (the definite article was later discarded). The supergroup's third LP, *Wheels of Fire*, was the world's first-ever platinum-selling double album. Cream burned brightly but briefly, going out with a bang with a farewell gig at the Royal Albert Hall in November 1968.

## PAUL McCARTNEY & WINGS
### Kings College Hospital, SE5

It's extremely rare that the naming of a band can be narrowed down to a single day. But the christening of McCartney's post-Beatles band is an exception. Paul and his wife Linda had been rehearsing for a while with the two Dennys – guitarist Denny Laine and drummer Denny Seiwell – when Linda was rushed to hospital here in Denmark Hill to give birth to the McCartneys' second child on 13 September, 1971. There were complications and, faced with the terrifying possibility that Linda and her baby might both perish, Paul sat outside the delivery room in King's College Hospital 'praying like mad'. Images of feathery angels' wings came unbidden to his mind, and he decided there and then that the band would be called Wings. Fortunately, Linda and the baby survived, and the couple named their new arrival Stella.

## ROXY MUSIC
### 21 Eversleigh Road, SW11

In the early 1970s this small terraced house in Battersea, not far from Clapham Junction, was shared by singer Bryan Ferry and woodwind player Andy Mackay, who joked about performing as a duo called the Eversleigh Brothers, after the name of the road. But the real band that was taking shape here was Roxy Music. Phil Manzanera came to this house to audition for the vacancy of guitarist, and found a setup comprising Ferry, Mackay, Brian Eno, drummer Paul Thompson and bassist Graham Simpson packed into a tiny room. Manzanera had a cold and was sneezing through the audition, which he failed. Later, he had another try – this time in a house in Colville Terrace, Notting Hill – and was accepted into the band.

# PERFORMANCES

Performing is what most rock 'n' roll stars do best; it's their *raison d'être*. This chapter explores many of the places in London – the clubs, the fancy halls, the open spaces and the dive bars – where they plugged in and made history. We also pinpoint the locations where notable videos and film clips were shot.

The 'video' for Bob Dylan's 'Subterranean Homesick Blues' was filmed in an alleyway close to The Savoy Hotel in 1965 (see page 90). *Moviestore/REX/Shutterstock*

# CENTRAL LONDON

## THE KINKS
**Lotus House restaurant,
61 Edgware Road, W2**

On New Year's Eve in 1963, a promising young London band called the Ravens played to diners eating Chinese food at the Lotus House restaurant. The band included brothers Ray and Dave Davies, and their managers Robert Wace and Grenville Collins were here with Arthur Howes, who often ate here and happened to be a booking agent for the Beatles. Howes liked the band's exuberant R&B and promptly added them to his roster of clients. But fame and fortune only arrived after the Ravens changed their name to the Kinks.

## BOB DYLAN
**Savoy Steps, Strand, WC2**

Dylan's famous promotional film for his single 'Subterranean Homesick Blues' was shot at the intersection of Savoy Hill Road and an alley known as the Savoy Steps, near the Savoy hotel, where he was staying at the time. The clip, which features the singer displaying parts of the song's lyric on a set of placards, is often cited as the earliest music 'video'. It was shot on 7 May, 1965, and was used as the opening sequence of DA Pennebaker's documentary film about Dylan in England, *Don't Look Back*.

## JIMI HENDRIX

**Saville Theatre,**
**135 Shaftesbury Avenue, WC2**

After the Saville Theatre was leased by the Beatles' manager, Brian Epstein, it became a rock venue as well as a playhouse. On Sunday, 4 June, 1967, Paul McCartney and George Harrison joined the audience here in Covent Garden to see a gig by the Jimi Hendrix Experience. The curtains opened and the group burst into their surprise opening number – 'Sgt Pepper's Lonely Hearts Club Band', from the Beatles' album that had been released three days earlier. McCartney later recalled being both flabbergasted and thrilled. 'It's a pretty major compliment in anyone's book,' he said. 'I put that down to one of the great honours of my career.' During the course of 1970, the Beatles officially split up, Jimi Hendrix passed away, and the Saville Theatre was turned into a cinema.

## PINK FLOYD

**Hyde Park**

Hyde Park's first free pop concert took place on 29 June, 1968, when Pink Floyd shared their trippy space rock with thousands of people in the sunshine. This was the mach-two version of the band, guitarist and vocalist David Gilmour having replaced Syd Barrett. The Floyd played just four numbers: 'Let There Be More Light', 'Set the Controls for the Heart of the Sun', 'A Saucerful of Secrets' and 'Interstellar Overdrive'. The DJ John Peel hired a boat, rowed into the middle of the Serpentine and lapped up the vibes. 'I think their music then suited the open air perfectly,' he enthused later. 'They just seemed to fill the whole sky and everything, and to coincide perfectly with the lapping of the water and the trees...' Also on the bill were Jethro Tull, Roy Harper and another Peel-endorsed act, Tyrannosaurus Rex, featuring a warbling, cross-legged Marc Bolan.

## THE ROLLING STONES

**Hyde Park**

The Stones rehearsed for their free Hyde Park bash in the Beatles' Apple studio in the basement of 3 Savile Row. But they subsequently parted ways with founder member Brian

More than 250,000 people watched the Rolling Stones' free concert in Hyde Park in July 1969.
*Trinity Mirror/ Mirrorpix/Alamy Stock Photo*

Jones, and the guitarist was tragically found dead just two days before they took the stage. Before the main event on Saturday, 5 July, 1969, a series of lesser-known bands entertained the crowd, including King Crimson, Family, the Third Ear Band and the Battered Ornaments. Finally, Mick Jagger appeared in his priestly white outfit, quoting Shelley's *Adonais* to mark the band's bereavement – 'Peace, peace, he is not dead, he doth not sleep/He hath awakened from the dream of life.' Their setlist included 'Jumpin' Jack Flash' and 'Honky Tonk Women', and new boy Mick Taylor shaped up well on guitar. The audience of at least 250,000 included Paul McCartney, Marianne Faithfull, Keith Moon, Germaine Greer and Viv Stanshall.

## MICK JAGGER
**15 Lowndes Square, SW1**

Much of the 1970 cult movie *Performance* was filmed in Belgravia, in this white stucco house owned by the businessman and former politician Leonard Plugge. The film featured Mick Jagger as an erstwhile rock star living with two women, one of whom was played by Keith Richards' girlfriend Anita Pallenberg. Not only are Jagger and Pallenberg said to have had an affair during filming, but it is often alleged that their sex scenes weren't simulated. Richards was certainly troubled by the situation, and sat brooding in his Bentley outside the house as the cameras rolled.

## THE BEATLES
**Apple Corps Headquarters,**
**3 Savile Row, W1**

People flocked to Savile Row when they heard live music coming from this rooftop at lunchtime on Thursday, 30 January, 1969. It took a while to confirm that it was the Beatles, for two main reasons: they weren't visible from the street below, and they were playing a batch of new songs ('Get Back', 'Don't Let Me Down', 'I've Got a Feeling' and 'Dig a Pony'), with an unfamiliar old number thrown in ('One after 909'). But this was the roof of their Apple Corps headquarters in Mayfair, and their voices and musical style were unmistakable. The Beatles (augmented by Billy Preston on electric piano) were supposed to be recording the finale to a TV special, but the 'rooftop concert' ended up as the conclusion to the film *Let It Be*. The 'noise nuisance' lasted about 42 minutes, ending after grumbles from local businesses and an amicable negotiation with the Metropolitan Police. It was the last time the group performed live in public.

## GENESIS
**Theatre Royal,**
**Drury Lane, WC2**

The Peter Gabriel-fronted incarnation of Genesis was arguably at its peak in 1973, when it released the acclaimed album *Selling England by the Pound* and took the new songs on tour. The prog-rockers were completely at home when they played the haunted old Theatre Royal in Covent Garden in January 1974. They played old crowd-pleasers, including the mammoth 'Supper's Ready', and the whimsical 'Harold the Barrel' made a surprise reappearance in their set. Gabriel remained in fine voice as he threw on a large wardrobe of fantasy costumes, appearing as Britannia for 'Dancing with the Moonlit Knight' and as the ghost of an old man for 'The Musical Box'. The following year it was 'all change' when he shocked fans by leaving the band.

## THE SEX PISTOLS
**Saint Martin's School of Art,**
**107-109 Charing Cross Road,**
**WC2**

The Pistols made their inauspicious live debut here on 6 November, 1975, when this was the site of Saint Martin's School of Art (their original bass player Glen Matlock was a student here at the time). It was too early for 'Anarchy in the U.K.' or 'God Save the Queen' – instead they played mostly covers including 'Substitute' by the Who, and 'Whatcha Gonna Do About It?' by the Small Faces. Drummer Paul Cook later remembered their performance as 'total chaos. We were very nervous and all over the place.' The band's thrashings were cut short after about 20 minutes, before

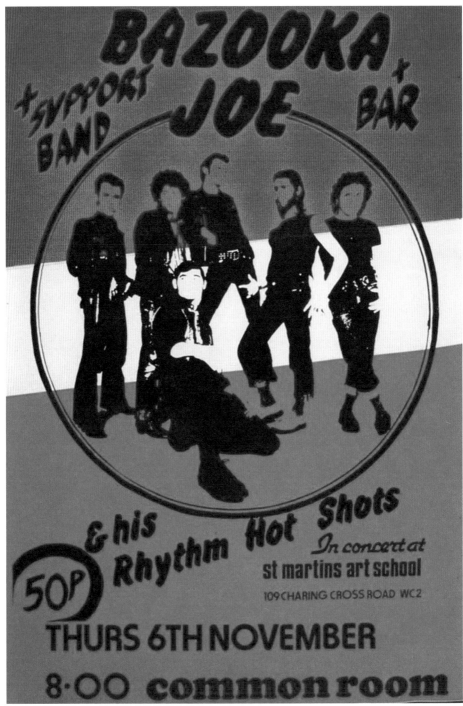

The Sex Pistols' first gig was as the 'support' for Bazooka Joe, a band that featured Stuart Goddard, later aka Adam Ant.

the evening's main act replaced them on stage. This was a slightly more competent band called Bazooka Joe, featuring a 21-year-old Stuart Goddard. Goddard, also a student at the college, would later become Adam Ant. The building eventually became the premises of Foyles bookshop, when it moved from nearby 121 Charing Cross Road.

## BOB MARLEY & THE WAILERS
**Lyceum Ballroom,**
**21 Wellington Street, WC2**

Tickets for Bob Marley's two shows at the Lyceum Ballroom, Covent Garden, in July 1977 were changing hands for small fortunes. Those lucky enough to attend had to endure stifling heat and clouds of exotic smoke, but it was worth it for the charged atmosphere and electrifying reggae. Fortunately, the music was recorded for the album *Live!*, thanks to a mobile studio provided by the Rolling Stones. The set yielded an unforgettable version of 'No Woman No Cry', which became an international hit. Marley had majestically metamorphosed from a cult artist into a global star.

## NIRVANA
**London Astoria,**
**157 Charing Cross Road, WC2**

The American grunge trio had played the London Astoria in December 1989, but they had been third on the bill, were exhausted from a long European tour, and hadn't impressed. When they returned here on 24 October, 1990, Nirvana were headlining and were an altogether different band – tight, powerful, and playing better songs. One reason for the transformation was their new drummer, Dave Grohl. In an interview after the show, singer and guitarist Kurt Cobain said they had been through half a dozen drummers but had finally found the perfect man, and even claimed that the band would split up if he left. Their classic album, *Nevermind*, appeared less than a year later. The much-loved Astoria has since been demolished.

Nirvana hanging out in Shepherd's Bush, October 1994. *Martyn Goodacre/Getty Images*

## BLUR
**Trafalgar Square, WC2**

The black-and-white video for Blur's 1993 single 'For Tomorrow', filmed by Julien Temple, includes many shots of Trafalgar Square, featuring Nelson's Column and a host of pigeons. Singer Damon Albarn leans out of a London bus, and we're suddenly transported north to Primrose Hill, where the band fly kites and Albarn rolls down a hill with a young lady.

## OASIS
**Royal Festival Hall,**
**Belvedere Road, SE1**

Britpop's finest came to the South Bank to play a set for *MTV Unplugged* on 23 August, 1996, during their tour to promote the album *(What's the Story) Morning Glory?* All seemed to be going reasonably well until Liam Gallagher suddenly pulled out of the gig, claiming to have a 'sore throat'. Instead of cancelling, brother Noel decided to carry on without him, assuming vocal duties for the evening. He did a fine job throughout the 90-minute show, despite loud Mancunian heckles from a certain member of the audience – Liam. It wasn't quite the kind of entertainment MTV had been expecting.

## ERIC CLAPTON
**Royal Albert Hall,**
**Kensington Gore, SW7**

The guitarist has played here so often that he has likened the hall to his 'front room'. His first gig at this classic Victorian venue was in 1964 with the Yardbirds. In November 1968 he was back in South Kensington with his supergroup Cream, playing two farewell concerts just before the band called it a day. And Clapton has subsequently played the Albert Hall on many occasions as a solo artist (including a record run of 24 nights in 1991), pushing his total appearances over the 200 mark. The hall has a capacity of over 5,000, so 'Slowhand' is likely to have entertained a million people here.

"LIAM AIN'T GONNA BE WITH US 'CAUSE HE'S GOT A SORE THROAT, SO YOU'RE STUCK WITH THE UGLY FOUR."

NOEL GALLAGHER, MTV UNPLUGGED AT THE ROYAL FESTIVAL HALL

# NORTH LONDON

## MUDDY WATERS
**St Pancras Town Hall,**
**96 Euston Road, NW1**

British jazzman Chris Barber brought Muddy to London in October 1958, and the Mississippi legend amazed the crowd in the Assembly Rooms at St Pancras Town Hall with his electric blues. He played 'I Can't Be Satisfied', 'I'm a Hoochie Coochie Man' and 'Long Distance Call' on his Fender Telecaster electric guitar, making many new fans but causing acoustic-blues purists to leave the hall. But an even bigger sound resulted when Muddy was backed by the Chris Barber Band on the classic 'Got My Mojo Working'. One reviewer wrote: 'By the time the spellbinding 'Blues Before Sunrise' came up, Muddy had the audience hooked on the end of those curling blue notes that shot, shimmering, from the big amplifier box.' St Pancras Town Hall was later renamed Camden Town Hall.

## THE WHO
**Railway Tavern,**
**High Street, Harrow, HA3**

The band were playing at this pub by Harrow & Wealdstone Tube station in September 1964 when Pete Townshend accidentally broke the headstock of his Rickenbacker electric guitar on the low ceiling. He quickly decided to finish the destruction of the instrument, later recounting: 'I thought I had no other recourse but to make it look like I had meant to do it, so I smashed this guitar and jumped all over the bits...' The guitarist then picked up his

Rickenbacker 12-string and continued playing as if nothing had happened. Townshend, and The Who in general, would become notorious for wrecking valuable equipment. It seems apt that the pub has since been demolished.

## ARETHA FRANKLIN
Finsbury Park Astoria,
232 Seven Sisters Road, N4

Studio and stage commitments kept Aretha from visiting London until May 1968, by which time she was a major star. Rapturous applause greeted the soul singer's British concert debut at Finsbury Park Astoria, where she delivered passionate renditions of 'Respect', '(You Make Me Feel Like a) Natural Woman' and the Stones' '(I Can't Get No) Satisfaction'. She enjoyed a similar reception at the Hammersmith Odeon, and commented: 'You know, I was rather surprised at the audience response in England. I rather thought they would enjoy the show. I didn't think they would enjoy it so much!' The Finsbury Park Astoria later became the Rainbow.

## THE CLASH
Rainbow,
232 Seven Sisters Road, N4

Formerly the Finsbury Park Astoria, the Rainbow became one of the most prestigious rock venues of the 1970s, hosting big names including David Bowie, Bob Marley, The Who, Roxy Music, Stevie Wonder, Pink Floyd, Queen and the Osmonds. In May 1977 it hosted one of the most infamous punk-rock gigs, when the Clash were supported by four other bands including the Jam and Buzzcocks. Joe Strummer and company played incandescent versions of 'London's Burning' and 'White Riot', and the singer introduced a cover of Junior Murvin's 'Police and Thieves' with the lines: 'Last week, 119,000 people voted National Front in London. Well, this next one's by a wog. And if you don't like wogs, you know where the bog is.' Excitable fans pogoed around and tore up the theatre's seats to make space, causing extensive damage. A fragment of iron from one of the seat frames – a missile

The Clash on stage at the Rainbow Theatre. *Andre Csillag/REX/Shutterstock*

that had narrowly missed Strummer on stage – found its way to a London auction in 2010, where it fetched £120. The Rainbow closed its doors to live music in 1981, becoming an occasional boxing venue before reopening as a Brazilian Pentecostal church.

## THE DOORS
**The Roundhouse,**
**Chalk Farm Road, NW1**

Astonishingly, this former train shed in Camden was the only British venue where the Doors ever performed live. They played four shows over one weekend here in September 1968, and were joined on the bill by Jefferson Airplane and the Crazy World of Arthur Brown. The morality campaigner Mary Whitehouse alerted Special Branch by telegram, warning: 'The Doors, who are a political extremist organisation, are now in England.' Jim Morrison and his band played favourites including 'Break on Through (to the Other Side)', 'Light My Fire' and 'The Unknown Soldier'. Although obviously stoned for much of the time, Morrison was impressed with the reception. 'The audience was one of the best we've ever had,' he said 'In the States they're there to enjoy themselves as much as they come to hear you. But at the Roundhouse they were there to listen. It was like going back to the roots. It stimulated us.'

## THE DAMNED
**Hope and Anchor pub,**
**207 Upper Street, N1**

The promotional video for the band's debut single, 'New Rose', widely regarded as Britain's first punk-rock record, was recorded in the famous Hope and Anchor pub in Islington on 7 December, 1976. The Damned's label, Stiff, arranged for a small camera team to capture the band on stage as they mimed to the recording.

# U2

## Hope and Anchor pub,
## 207 Upper Street, N1

On 4 December, 1979, the Irish band played their first London gig at the Hope and Anchor, renowned for its punk-rock connections. Lead singer Bono Vox had told *Record Mirror*: 'I want people in London to see and hear the band. I want to replace the bands in the charts now, because I think we're better.' (The bands in the charts back then included Styx, the Eagles and Dr Hook.) Mistakenly billed as 'The U2's', Bono and company failed to complete their set, leaving the stage after The Edge accidentally broke a guitar string. U2 had a better time at their next London gig, at the Rock Garden in Covent Garden – though they could have bombed, having been billed this time as 'V2'.

# MADONNA

## Camden Palace,
## 1A Camden High Street, NW1

When Madonna Ciccone was launched on London in October 1983, it wasn't with a proper concert, but with a 'track date' in Camden Town. The 25-year-old singer, from Michigan via New York, performed a few songs to backing tracks at the Camden Palace, pricking up the ears of jaded critics. One wrote: 'Dressed in holocaust chic – black top, black skirt and leggings, lots of bare midriff, and hair in ringlets – she sang well, with a husky, black-sounding voice, and danced even better. She hurtled around the stage, mostly swivelling her hips like a belly-dancer...' In 2004 the Camden Palace was revitalised and renamed KOKO.

# MADNESS

## Islip Street, Kentish Town,
## NW5

The video for the 1980 hit 'Baggy Trousers' was shot in the grounds of a primary school in this street near Kentish Town Tube station. It features the band's saxophone player Lee Thompson 'flying' through the air – with the aid of wires suspended from a crane.

# Starfish

## + others

**Friday 16th January,**

live at

## The Laurel Tree,
Camden.

**Bar till 2 a.m**

**Entrance £4 with a flyer.**

The flyer for Coldplay's first incarnation, Starfish, distributed around the streets of Camden in January 1998.

## COLDPLAY
**Laurel Tree pub,
113 Bayham Street, NW1**

Chris Martin and his embryonic band performed their first-ever gig in January 1998 upstairs in the Laurel Tree pub in Camden Town, not far from the flat that Martin shared with guitarist Jonny Buckland at 268 Camden Road. They hadn't settled on a band name, and quickly chose 'Starfish'. It was just £4 to enter if you came with a flyer advertising the gig, and the place was packed because they had alerted many of their friends. Starfish played just six songs, and none of them was 'Yellow'.

## ROBERT FRIPP
**Union Chapel,
Compton Terrace, N1**

On 31 May, 1997, the 51-year-old King Crimson guitarist settled down in this serene Congregational church in Islington to play one of the longest concerts given by a solo musician. Armed with his Gibson Les Paul guitar and a stack of 'Frippertronics', Toyah Willcox's famous husband filled the building with squalling, tinkling, ethereal and mellifluous sounds between 12 noon and 8pm – pausing periodically to distribute cups of coffee and biscuits to members of the audience with the longest attention spans.

## TAYLOR SWIFT
**Bull and Gate pub,
389 Kentish Town Road, NW5**

The video for the single 'End Game' was shot in Miami, Tokyo and London in 2017, and the London segment shows the American star at the Bull and Gate, a lovely old pub in Kentish Town. Swift and her friends are seen partying in the pub's Boulogne Bar, known for its fancy cocktails. She can also be seen in nearby Falkland Place, off Falkland Road (unwittingly near the site where Madness filmed 'Baggy Trousers'), and – much further away – on the Millennium Bridge, with St Paul's Cathedral in the background.

# WEST LONDON

## THE SOUND OF MOTOWN

**Rediffusion Studios,
128 Wembley Park Drive, HA9**

The cream of Motown Records came to Wembley on 18 March, 1965, to record a TV spectacular at Rediffusion Studios. *The Sound of Motown*, a special edition of *Ready Steady Go!*, was presented by soul fan Dusty Springfield and starred the Supremes, Martha and the Vandellas, Smokey Robinson and the Miracles, the Temptations, and Little Stevie Wonder. Among the classic songs performed in this hangar-like space were 'Dancing in the Street', 'Stop! In the Name of Love' and 'You've Really Got a Hold on Me'. There was a momentary crisis during the recording when Diana Ross went missing, but she was eventually found dozing backstage. The TV show turned countless British people on to the music of the Detroit label.

## THE BEATLES

**5-11 Ailsa Avenue, TW1**

Four adjoining houses here in St Margarets, Twickenham, play a memorable part in the 1965 movie *Help!* When the Beatles alight from a Rolls-Royce in this avenue, they go through the four front doors – Ringo entering No. 5, John No. 7, Paul No. 9 and George No. 11. Through the magic of cinema, they emerge in a big communal living space (actually created at Twickenham Studios).

## DAVID BOWIE

**Hammersmith Odeon,
45 Queen Caroline Street, W6**

Bowie was playing the Hammersmith Odeon on 3 July, 1973, when he made a shock stage announcement. 'This show will stay the longest in our memories,' he said. 'Not just because it is the end of the tour, but because it is the last show we'll ever do.' Confusion reigned: people thought he was quitting as an artist – that Bowie would never sing live again. But what he was actually doing was killing off his Ziggy Stardust character. He'd played the alien-rock-star part over more than a year of touring, and it was time for new creative challenges. He was also retiring his band, the Spiders from Mars – and the stage announcement was the first they'd heard about it. No wonder they looked slightly dazed as they burst into 'Rock 'n' Roll Suicide'.

## KATE BUSH

**Hammersmith Apollo,
45 Queen Caroline Street, W6**

When Kate Bush announced a return to the stage in 2014 after a break of 35 years, fans snapped up the tickets within minutes, and the original run of 15 gigs at the Hammersmith Apollo expanded to a 22-night run. Her elaborate multimedia show, *Before the Dawn*, included puppets, 3D animation and other illusions, and the 56-year-old singer performed the whole of 'The Ninth Wave' from her *Hounds of Love* album and the second side of *Aerial* – but nothing at all from her first four albums, not even 'Wuthering Heights'. It didn't stop fans and reviewers from going into raptures.

## RICK WAKEMAN

**Wembley Arena,
Engineers Way, HA9**

The ambitious keyboard wizard turned to Camelot for his third solo album, *The Myths and Legends of King Arthur and the Knights of the Round Table*. He fancied playing gigs at Tintagel Castle in Cornwall, but when permission wasn't forthcoming he settled for three dates at Wembley Arena from the end of May 1975. There was just one hitch: the arena was about to host the *Ice Follies*, so it had become a huge frozen rink. Wakeman decided to go

RMAN Presents

# ROBERT FORSTER

+ Special Guests

~~FRIDAY 7th OCTOBER 1994~~

L.A. 2 (LONDON
5 Charing C

CLUB SPANGLE PRESENTS

## blur

at
**THE DUBLIN CASTLE**
94 PARKWAY CAMDEN, LONDON

**Thursday 18th May 1**
TICKETS £6    DOORS 8pm

RA

AFT

24 0

OK COMPUT

METROPOLIS MUSIC present

# EDWYN
## CO

CHARING

NUMBER
AIRS – STAND

MEAN FIDDLER PRES
THE GO-BETWEENS
GUES

TICKET NUMBER

UNRESERVED PLACE    4    7

A-TYPE

THE GARAGE PRE

ROPOLIS MUSIC PRESENTS

# ndersticks

### THE FORUM
**nday 1st May 1995**
Doors Time: 7.00 p.m.
ket Price: £8.50 (Advance)

STANDING DOWNSTAIRS    000578

Metropolis Musi
# Nick Cave & The B

Doors 7
U15s with a

## Hammersmith
## Saturday 26

Stalls S

STANDING
TICKET

£ 16 5

£ 16 5

presents
# The La's
## SUNDAY 18 NOVEMBER 1990

town & country club
9-17 Highgate Road, Kentish Town, London NW5
Doors: 7.30pm  Admission: £6 Advance

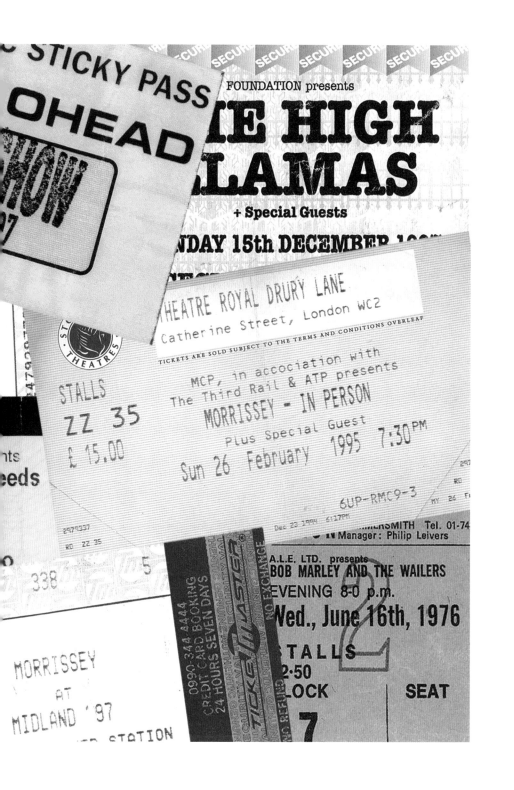

STICKY PASS

OHEAD

SHOW

'97

FOUNDATION presents

THE HIGH
LLAMAS

+ Special Guests

MONDAY 15th DECEMBER 1997

THEATRE ROYAL DRURY LANE
Catherine Street, London WC2

TICKETS ARE SOLD SUBJECT TO THE TERMS AND CONDITIONS OVERLEAF

MCP, in accociation with
The Third Rail & ATP presents

MORRISSEY - IN PERSON

Plus Special Guest

Sun 26 February 1995 7:30PM

6UP-RMC9-3

Dec 23 1994  6:17PM

STOLL
THEATRES

STALLS

ZZ 35

£ 15.00

nts

eeds

2979337

RO ZZ 35

338

5

MORRISSEY
AT
MIDLAND '97

POWER STATION

A.L.E. LTD. presents

BOB MARLEY AND THE WAILERS

EVENING 8-0 p.m.

Wed., June 16th, 1976

STALLS

2-50

BLOCK

7

SEAT

0990-344-4444
CREDIT CARD BOOKING
24 HOURS SEVEN DAYS

TICKETMASTER

NO EXCHANGE · NO REFUND

HAMMERSMITH  Tel. 01-74

Manager : Philip Leivers

MY 26 F

ahead and stage his production on ice. Skaters wearing fake horse costumes slid around to his grandiose tunes, and a total of 27,000 punters witnessed one of the strangest rock shows of all time.

## DONNA SUMMER & MUSICAL YOUTH
### Bonner Hill Road, KT1

The Queen of Disco and the junior reggae stars came to a crumbling old girls' school here in Kingston-upon-Thames to film their video for the single 'Unconditional Love' in 1983. Summer played a sober schoolmistress who suddenly strips down to a spangly costume and leads a pack of children into the spacious playground for a spot of singing and dancing. The Edwardian brick school building has since been demolished.

## LIVE AID
### Wembley Stadium, Stadium Way, HA9

A *Who's Who* of British pop talent assembled here at the behest of Bob Geldof and Midge Ure on 13 July, 1985, to raise funds for famine relief in Ethiopia. Status Quo kicked off the 'global jukebox' with 'Rockin' All Over the World', and there were short sets from Bryan Ferry, David Bowie, Sade and Spandau Ballet. Phil Collins played here before flying by helicopter and Concorde (those were the days) to the parallel Live Aid event in Philadelphia. But the day ultimately belonged to Queen, who made something of a comeback, with Freddie Mercury playing the 72,000-strong audience like a musical instrument. Princess Diana and Paula Yates were in attendance, and the occasion climaxed with Paul McCartney singing 'Let It Be' before a starry ensemble including Geldof, Bowie, George Michael, Sting, Bono and Roger Daltrey launched wearily into 'Do They Know It's Christmas?' Bowie said he'd be happy to do this every year.

**WEMBLEY STADIUM**

MEL BUSH PRESENTS

**WHAM! THE FINAL**

TURNSTILES

**B**

PLUS SUPPORT

**SATURDAY, 28 JUNE, 1986**

GATES OPEN AT 2 p.m.

Concert starts approx. 4 p.m.

Subject to Licence

**TICKETS £13.50** INCL. VAT

6899

TO BE RETAINED     ISSUED SUBJECT TO THE CONDITIONS ON BACK

Nick Heywood and Gary Glitter were among the support acts for Wham!'s final gig.
*Photograph by Badgreeb Records/creativecommons.org/licenses/by-sa/3.0/legalcode*

# WHAM!

## Wembley Stadium,
## Stadium Way, HA9

In June 1986, just four years after releasing their debut single, Wham! called it a day with a single farewell concert at Wembley. Many of the 80,000-strong audience sang along as George Michael, Andrew Ridgeley and their band romped through their catalogue of hits for the last time. Elton John arrived on stage to accompany George as he covered 'Candle in the Wind', and Simon Le Bon joined in with the encore, 'I'm Your Man'. After the final screams died away, George Michael's earnest and troubled solo career got under way.

# MICHAEL JACKSON
**Wembley Stadium,**
**Stadium Way, HA9**

Jackson played seven gigs at Wembley in July 1988 as part of his first-ever solo concert tour, to promote his album *Bad*. The 29-year-old singer was at his peak, performing hits including 'Thriller', 'Billie Jean' and 'Beat It' and combining captivating vocal performances with dazzling dance routines. The show on 16 July was attended by Prince Charles and Princess Diana, and Jackson met Diana before the show. She asked him if he would be playing his song 'Dirty Diana', and he said he had removed it from the set out of respect for her. When she replied that it was her favourite song, he put it back in. The Wembley shows were watched by a record-breaking total of 504,000 people.

# ROXY MUSIC
**Riverside Studios,**
**Crisp Road, W6**

After a live absence of more than 18 years, Roxy returned with a special televised gig at these Hammersmith studios on 23 May, 2001. The BBC allotted free tickets to a select crowd of lucky fans. 'These tickets are like gold dust,' announced the Beeb, urging them to show their appreciation for the band 'by putting on your hippest clothes and dancing all evening.' They obliged as Bryan Ferry and his reassembled ensemble tore through old favourites including 'Virginia Plain', 'Love Is the Drug', 'Out of the Blue' and 'Do the Strand'. 'The Great Paul Thompson', absent from the Roxy drum stool since 1980, was back in his rightful place, and new member Lucy Wilkins impressed on violin and keyboards. Roxy's previous concert had been on 10 February, 1983, at Tokyo's Budokan Hall.

# THE DIXIE CHICKS

## Shepherd's Bush Empire, Shepherd's Bush Green, W12

The USA was on the verge of invading Iraq when the hugely popular Texan country trio played here in March 2003. 'Just so you know, we're on the good side with y'all,' lead singer Natalie Maines announced on stage. 'We do not want this war, this violence, and we're ashamed that the president of the United States is from Texas.' Everything was cool until right-wingers in the home country got wind of her remark, and then it was like John Lennon comparing the Beatles to Jesus all over again. The Chicks received death threats, their songs were wiped from the airwaves, and their CDs were bought in large quantities so they could be bulldozed.

# LONDON'S LOST CLUBS

## Some of the legendary bars and dives that helped to create London's diverse music scene

**THE 2 I'S COFFEE BAR, 59 Old Compton Street, W1:** Seminal venue for skiffle and rock 'n' roll. Tommy Steele and Cliff Richard grooved here.

**THE SCENE CLUB, Ham Yard, 41 Great Windmill Street, W1:** Hugely popular with mods, this basement club was the place to hear and dance to R&B, soul and blues records, including tracks by Chuck Berry, Bo Diddley, Howlin' Wolf and James Brown. Bands including The Who and the Animals also performed here.

**TIN PAN ALLEY CLUB, 7 Denmark Street, WC2:** Originally a 17th-century terraced house, this became a hip watering hole in the heart of London's music district. Assorted rockers were photographed outside the club, including Bill Haley, the Rolling Stones (see cover) and Malcolm McLaren.

**THE FLAMINGO CLUB, 33-37 Wardour Street, W1:** Meeting place for music-loving mods and famous musicians including the Beatles and the Stones. It not only featured rock and R&B bands, but was one of the first places to introduce Jamaican ska music to white audiences.

**BAG O'NAILS, 9 Kingly Street, W1:** Basement club where the Beatles, the Stones and Hendrix hung out. Paul McCartney met his future wife Linda here in 1967.

**THE MARQUEE, 90 Wardour Street, W1:** London's most famous rock club, whose stage was occupied by countless big name acts including David Bowie, Led Zeppelin, Jethro Tull, Rory Gallagher, the Stranglers, the Police, Prince, Iron Maiden, Dire Straits and the Cure.

**UFO, 31 Tottenham Court Road, W1; The Roundhouse, Chalk Farm Road, NW1:** Club for underground music and hippie happenings, known for combining sounds with trippy light shows. Pink Floyd, Soft Machine and Procol Harum were among the bands who played here. Initially based underneath a cinema in Tottenham Court Road, the club later moved to the Roundhouse in Camden.

**MIDDLE EARTH, 43 King Street, WC2:** Its name inspired by the works of Tolkien, this Covent Garden club hosted bands including Pink Floyd, the Move, Captain Beefheart and Tyrannosaurus Rex. People enjoyed themselves so much here that it was often the target of police drug raids.

**SPEAKEASY, 48-50 Margaret Street, W1:** West End haunt of Bowie, Clapton, Hendrix, The Who, the Sex Pistols, the Clash and gossiping music journalists.

**SOMBRERO, 142 Kensington High Street, W8:** Gay club (whose real name was Yours Or Mine) in the basement of Mexican restaurant El Sombrero. Popular with early-'70s glam-rockers.

**THE ROXY, 41-43 Neal Street, WC2:** A former gay club that was transformed into the home of punk rock in late 1976.

**VORTEX, 201 Wardour Street, W1:** Short-lived punk club where bands including Buzzcocks, Siouxsie and the Banshees, and the Slits played. Later became a mod-revival hangout, then a disco and dance club.

**BLITZ, 4 Great Queen Street, WC2:** Hotspot for the burgeoning New Romantic movement. Gary Kemp of Spandau Ballet dubbed it 'Studio 54 in London for the poor'.

# EAST
# LONDON

## IRON MAIDEN
**Cart & Horses pub,
1 Maryland Point, E15**

The Cart & Horses pub in Stratford was the birthplace of Iron Maiden, who played here many times from the mid-1970s with a series of shifting lineups. The band played early versions of the numbers 'Iron Maiden', 'Prowler' and 'Wrathchild' to packed houses here. After Maiden graduated to the stadiums, the pub became a shrine and a place of pilgrimage for men in black T-shirts shouting 'Up the Irons!'

## THE VERVE
**Hoxton Street, N1**

The video for the 1997 single 'Bitter Sweet Symphony' shows the Verve's lead singer Richard Ashcroft walking determinedly down this road in fashionable Hoxton with a shocking lack of regard for fellow pedestrians. Ashcroft begins his walk near the junction of Hoxton Street and Falkirk Street, and continues north on Hoxton Street. He is eventually joined by the remainder of the band. The concept was inspired by the video for Massive Attack's similarly titled 'Unfinished Sympathy', which was set in Los Angeles.

## ARCTIC MONKEYS
**Howl At The Moon pub,
178 Hoxton Street, N1**

The video for the 2013 single 'Why'd You Only Call Me When You're High' begins with the Sheffield band at the Howl At The Moon pub, at the junction of Hoxton Street and Stanway Street. Lead singer Alex Turner sends text messages while spaced out and hallucinating, seeing the hands on the clock take on a life of their own. He leaves the pub and wanders the streets, still experiencing peculiar visions, heading for a doomed assignation with a young woman.

# GOLDFRAPP

**Spitz,**
**109 Commercial Street,**
**Spitalfields, E1**

Alison Goldfrapp and Will Gregory introduced their innovative electronic music to Londoners at the Spitz on 5 October, 2000, shortly after the release of their first album, *Felt Mountain*. Reviewers were wowed by their sound, hearing echoes of film music and of acts as diverse as Portishead, Massive Attack, Billie Holiday and Shirley Bassey. But the lead singer – later widely acknowledged as Britain's foremost electro diva – had yet to perfect her stage persona. One critic, while finding her vocals 'spellbinding', wrote: 'Between songs Alison Goldfrapp just stalks the small stage. Petulant, distracted, self-conscious, she looks like she's been waiting for a bus in the rain for hours.'

# PRINCE

**O2 Arena,**
**Greenwich Peninsula, SE10**

Fans filing into the O2 between August and September 2007 knew they were in for something special when they saw the big stage in the middle of the arena, fashioned in the shape of the curly symbol that had once replaced Prince's name. The Purple One had reportedly rehearsed about 130 songs before playing his landmark residency here (*21 Nights in London: The Earth Tour*), and none of the sets were alike. He and his super-tight, effortlessly funky band reeled off familiar hits including 'Purple Rain', '1999', 'When Doves Cry' and 'Kiss', and threw in more obscure numbers and fragments for more dedicated aficionados. He also covered Chic, Gnarls Barkley, Louis Armstrong, the Rolling Stones and the Beatles. The air of unpredictability only added to the excitement; one night, Elton John hopped up on stage to duet on 'The Long and Winding Road'.

The Arctic Monkeys' video for 'Why'd You Only Call Me When You're High' begins in a Hoxton pub.
*Andy Willsher/Redferns/Getty Images*

# S O U T H  L O N D O N

## DAVID BOWIE
**Green Man pub,**
**1 Dartmouth Row, SE10**

One evening in 1963, a band called the Konrads were due to play a gig at the Green Man pub on this site in Blackheath. But as he was changing into his stage clothes, the lead singer, Roger Ferris, stepped on a broken glass and severely injured his foot. He was taken to hospital, and others decided to play with out him. Another member of the band, David Jones, stepped into the breach and became the lead singer that night. It was one more learning experience in an unusually long musical apprenticeship. Lasting fame would arrive less than a decade later, by which time he had changed his name to David Bowie. The pub was demolished long ago.

## KATE BUSH
**Rose of Lee pub,**
**162 Lee High Road, SE13**

Bush made her stage debut at the Rose of Lee pub in Lewisham one evening in March 1977, fronting the short-lived KT Bush Band, which included her future collaborator and boyfriend Del Palmer on bass. The audience was small and largely indifferent and the diminutive singer was nervous, and she and the band received £27 for their efforts. But she was already signed to EMI, and by the following year would be the talk of the nation when her debut single 'Wuthering Heights' rocketed to No. 1. The pub later became the Dirty South bar and restaurant.

## DIRE STRAITS
### Farrer House, Deptford
### Church Street, SE8

Dire Straits didn't travel very far for their live debut. In the summer of 1977, when most of the band were living in this block of council flats, guitarists Mark and David Knopfler, bassist John Illsley and drummer Pick Withers played their first gig to a small audience as part of an informal open-air festival outside the building. Electricity came from a single power cable that snaked all the way to a wall socket inside one of the flats.

## ROCK AGAINST RACISM CARNIVAL
### Brockwell Park, SE24

On 24 September, 1978, the Rock Against Racism (RAR) campaign attracted 100,000 people to Brockwell Park, south of Brixton, in a show of defiance against far-right organisations such as the National Front. Many wore RAR and Anti-Nazi League badges, but they were also here to enjoy some great music. The British bands Misty in Roots and Aswad soothed the crowd with cool reggae, and Stiff Little Fingers delivered a blast of Belfast punk rock. Elvis Costello and the Attractions ended the event with a storming set, which began with Costello announcing: 'Welcome to the Black and White Minstrel Show! How about jumping up and down against racism?' This was the second RAR carnival in London, the first having featured the Clash, the Tom Robinson Band and Steel Pulse in Victoria Park, Hackney.

## DEXYS MIDNIGHT RUNNERS
### Brook Drive, SE11

Much of the video for Dexys' 1982 chart-topper 'Come On Eileen' was filmed in Kennington, at the corner of Brook Drive and Hayles Street, near Elephant and Castle. Kevin Rowland and the band pranced around in their dungarees here until darkness fell. Also visible is nearby Holyoak Road, off Dante Road. The character of Eileen – who also appears with Rowland on the artwork of the record sleeve – was played by Máire Fahey, the sister of Siobhan Fahey of Bananarama.

# "SOUTH LONDON FOREVER"

FLORENCE + THE MACHINE

## GOLDFRAPP
**Addington Square, SE5**

The video for Goldfrapp's 2008 single 'Happiness' was shot in this Camberwell square, on the edge of Burgess Park. Featuring a young man jumping around in a white suit, the video also stars Alison Goldfrapp and her bandmate Will Gregory in various guises. She plays a policewoman, a flower seller and a topiarist, while he plays a postman and a street-sweeper. The video is a homage to a street-dancing scene in the 1953 movie *Small Town Girl*.

## FLORENCE + THE MACHINE
**Joiners Arms pub,**
**35 Denmark Hill, SE5**

One hot afternoon in July 2018, it was announced that Florence Welch was about to play an intimate gig at the Joiners Arms pub in Camberwell. Hundreds of fans of Florence + The Machine converged and formed a queue on Denmark Hill, and a lucky throng were admitted to the back room, where Welch – accompanied by guitarist Rob Ackroyd and harpist Tom Monger – played elegantly stripped-down versions of her songs, including 'Sky Full of Song', 'Cosmic Love' and 'Dog Days Are Over'. There were loud cheers when the Camberwell-born star sang 'South London Forever' (from her 2018 album *High as Hope*), which name-checks this very pub.

## GARBAGE
**Brixton Academy,**
**211 Stockwell Road, SW9**

In 2018, Shirley Manson and her American chums celebrated the 20th anniversary of their searing sophomore album, *Version 2.0*, with the 20 Years Paranoid tour. At Brixton Academy in mid-September they sounded better than ever, with their futuristic techno-grunge cranked up by 21st-century technology. All 12 tracks, from the blasting singalong of 'Temptation Waits' to a sublime extended version of 'You Look So Fine', were supplemented by fan-pleasing B-sides from the period, plus their epic 1999 James Bond theme, 'The World Is Not Enough'. Manson sang like a diva half her age and prowled the stage in a flowing red dress, looking 'like the Bride of Frankenstein', according to one audience member.

# RECORDINGS

Thanks to all the people who created tape machines and mixing desks, we can transcend time and space whenever we like: we can listen to all kinds of music that was made decades ago, and we can choose the locations where we listen to it. But the places where some of these songs were recorded are special in their own right. London has had many studios, some of them in unusual converted buildings, from old schools and churches to disused factories and power stations, and countless great singles and albums have been recorded here. And because records have historically needed protective wrappers, giving many of them visual appeal as well as sonic value, we can pinpoint the places where important album covers were created.

The ball and biscuit mic at Toe Rag Studios inspired a White Stripes song (see page 155). *Photograph Richard Ecclestone*

# CENTRAL LONDON

## THE ROLLING STONES
**Olympic Sound Studios, Carlton Street, SW1**

The Stones came to Olympic Sound Studios on this site off Regent Street to record their debut single, 'Come On', on 10 May, 1963, a week after the band was signed to Decca Records. The catchy little beat number was written by one of their heroes, Chuck Berry, and their version was produced by manager Andrew Loog Oldham. The same sessions yielded the B-side, 'I Wanna Be Loved'. The dilapidated 18th-century studio building, Carlton Hall, had previously been a synagogue. Olympic moved to new premises in Barnes in 1964, and the building was demolished to make way for a car park.

## THE KINKS
**Pye Studios, 40 Bryanston Street, W1**

Brothers Ray and Dave Davies and their band were so fond of Pye Studios, on the corner of Great Cumberland Place, that they spent many of their late nights and early mornings here in the 1960s, recording everything from the riffy 'All Day and All of the Night' to the majestic 'Waterloo Sunset' and the eccentric *The Kinks Are the Village Green Preservation Society*. Other acts who recorded at Pye included The Who ('I Can't Explain'), the Searchers ('Needles and Pins'), Petula Clark ('Downtown'), Status Quo ('Pictures of Matchstick Men') and Mungo Jerry ('In the Summertime').

# PYE STUDIOS

## THE ANIMALS
### 129 Kingsway, WC2

The British band had been trying out a hoary and mysterious old folk song, 'The House of the Rising Sun', on a 1964 tour, and it had gone down so well that they decided to record it as a potential hit single. They caught an early-morning train back to London, pushed their instruments through the streets on a British Rail handcart to De Lane Lea Studios, and nailed the number in two takes. It topped the charts in the UK and in the US, where its original lyric about a New Orleans whorehouse is likely to have been written.

## THE BEATLES
### Chelsea Manor Studios, 1-11 Flood Street, SW3

Some people assume that the cover of *Sgt Pepper's Lonely Hearts Club Band* was made as a flat collage, using glue and small cutouts of celebrities. In fact, the cutouts were lifesized and were positioned three-dimensionally in an art studio. Old waxworks of the band from Madame Tussauds were also positioned in the space, and the Beatles themselves posed at the centre of the whole assemblage, which was then photographed. The album cover was the creation of the pop artist Peter Blake and his then wife Jann Haworth, and the photographs were taken here in 1967 by Michael Cooper at his studio on the ground floor of Chelsea Manor Studios, just off the King's Road.

## THE WHO
### IBC Studios, 35 Portland Place, W1

The double album *Tommy* was mostly recorded at IBC Studios from late 1968 to early 1969. The studios, tucked amid the foreign embassies of Portland Place, were chosen by Who manager Kit Lambert because they were cheap, so the band could afford to spend several weeks here realising Pete Townshend's ambitious 'rock opera' about a boy rendered deaf, dumb and blind after a traumatic event. Townshend played keyboards as well as guitar, bassist John Entwistle added French horn, trumpet and flugelhorn, and Keith Moon was let loose on some timpani. This was the perfect building for unusual projects: during World War II

De Lane Lea studios currently resides in Dean Street, Soho; the Animals, the Beatles and others recorded at the studio's Kingsway home in the 1960s. *Cjc13/creativecommons.org/licenses/by-sa/3.0/legalcode*

it had housed a top-secret laboratory for the Special Operations Executive. (The song 'Pinball Wizard' was a late addition to the rock opera, and was recorded separately at Morgan Studios in Willesden.)

## DAVID BOWIE
**Trident Studios,**
**17 St Anne's Court, W1**

In 1969 the former David Jones recorded 'Space Oddity' at Trident Studios, tucked away in this alleyway off Wardour Street in Soho. The record, released in the year of the moon landing, would give him a tantalising burst of fame before he returned to the shadows. But Bowie was back at Trident the following year to record part of his album *The Man Who Sold the World*, and again in 1971 to record *Hunky Dory*. His next project would be *The Rise and Fall of Ziggy Stardust and the Spiders from Mars*, recorded here in the winter of 1971-72, after which there would be no return to obscurity for the Starman. He returned to Trident in the summer of '72 to produce Lou Reed's most listenable album, *Transformer*, featuring 'Walk on the Wild Side', 'Satellite of Love' and 'Perfect Day'. The Beatles had come to the studios in 1968 to record 'Hey Jude' as well as a few tracks for their White Album.

## SLADE
**Command Studios,**
**201 Piccadilly, W1**

The boys from the Black Country had scored a few hit singles when they came to Command Studios in the West End in October 1971 to record their next album. Aiming to capture their rip-roaring live sound, Slade played three consecutive nights here to a studio audience. The result was *Slade Alive!*, which contained mostly cover versions. Their interpretation of the Lovin' Spoonful song 'Darling Be Home Soon' included an inadvertent boozy belch from singer Noddy Holder, which he was later obliged to replicate when they played it on stage. The LP, which had cost just £600 to record, peaked at No. 2 in the UK charts. Command Studios had previously been a BBC studio, and back in the 1940s had been the Stage Door Canteen, where stars including Fred Astaire and Bing Crosby came to entertain men and women from the Forces.

## ROXY MUSIC
**Command Studios,
201 Piccadilly, W1**

Bryan Ferry and his motley band of art-rockers recorded their ground-breaking debut album in the basement at Command Studios in March 1972. It was a speculative recording, paid for by their management company, as they didn't yet have a record deal. The album was produced by Pete Sinfield, who was more at home writing airy-fairy lyrics for King Crimson than for recording bands. After a contract was signed with Island Records and the album was released, Roxy returned to Command to tape their debut single, 'Virginia Plain', which included the sound of a motorcycle revved up by a roadie along Piccadilly. Command Studios didn't last much longer, becoming a branch of the chemist chain Boots before the façade was demolished. The revamped site was later occupied by a hairdressing salon.

## DAVID BOWIE
**23 Heddon Street, W1**

Bowie posed here in 1972, just off Regent Street, for the cover of *The Rise and Fall of Ziggy Stardust and The Spiders from Mars*. The sign 'K West' denoted the headquarters of a fur business, which has long since packed its bags. On the back cover, the singer can be seen in a traditional red telephone box that once stood on the same street. For a short time after Bowie's death in 2016, No. 23 became the location of a spontaneous shrine created by fans, featuring hundreds of photographs and messages of mourning and remembrance. A wall plaque here still honours his memory.

David Bowie at Trident Studios, May 1970. *Rolf Adlercreutz/Alamy Stock Photo*

## THE JAM
**Polydor Records,
17-19 Stratford Place, W1**

Polydor Records had a studio here, just off Oxford Street, and this is where The Jam knocked off their debut album, *In the City*, in a matter of 11 days in March 1977. Paul Weller, Bruce Foxton and Rick Buckler tore through ten hooky, energetic numbers, which included the theme from the *Batman* TV series of the 1960s (Weller reportedly had a Batman poster on his bedroom wall as a boy). Critics said the results were promising but rushed, as if the band had been pushed into a studio before they were truly ready. The Jam paid no heed, hurrying into Basing Street Studios a few months later to record the sequel. The Clash also came to Stratford Place to make some rough-and-ready recordings in November 1976.

## IAN DURY
**Workhouse Studios,
488-490 Old Kent Road, SE1**

'Workhouse Studios in the Old Kent Road' has an Ian Dury ring about it, and the place certainly suited his music. He recorded his 1977 album, *New Boots and Panties!!,* here, and returned to create his masterful chart-topping single 'Hit Me with Your Rhythm Stick'. Dury and the Blockheads returned to cut the 1979 album *Do It Yourself* here, and the wordy hit 'Reasons to be Cheerful (Part 3)'. Manfred Mann's Earth Band also recorded their albums at Workhouse in the 1970s.

## IAN DURY
**Vauxhall Bridge Road, SW1**

The cover of *New Boots and Panties!!* shows Dury and his five-year-old son Baxter outside a long-lost clothing shop, Axfords, near Victoria station. A branch of Woolworth's – also gone – can be seen reflected in the shop window. Baxter later explained the image: 'I remember that Dad had an obsession about that shop; he continually talked about it and wanted to use it. But I wasn't meant to be in that picture: it was a complete accident. I remember standing on the other side of the street with the photographer's assistant and some equipment, and I was a bit shy and confused by

IAN DURY NEW BOOTS AND PANTIES!!

The cover of Ian Dury's 1977 album, *New Boots and Panties!!*, released on Stiff Records, was shot on Vauxhall Bridge Road. *TheCoverVersion/Alamy Stock Photo*

all the people, so I just walked up to Dad. That's why I've got a slightly shy "What am I doing here?" look.'

## KATE BUSH
**Air Studios,**
**214 Oxford Street, W1**

The teenage Catherine Bush from Bexleyheath recorded most of her debut album, *The Kick Inside*, in 1977 at AIR Studios above the bustle of Oxford Circus, aided by producer Andrew Powell and a crowd of session musicians. One of the tracks, 'The Man with the Child in His Eyes', was recorded two years earlier, when she was just 16. The album's 13 original compositions marked her out as a precocious talent, although not every critic was impressed – a reviewer in *Sounds* complained that 'some of the worst lyrics ever' were being delivered by 'the most irritatingly yelping voice since Robert Plant'. The album included 'Wuthering Heights', which became the first entirely self-composed song by a female artist to top the UK singles charts. As the musicians played and the technicians fiddled with microphones and sound effects, Kate Bush watched carefully: before long her music would be routinely self-produced.

# THE CLASH
**CBS Studios,**
**31-37 Whitfield Street, W1**

The band recorded their self-titled debut album in Studio Three of CBS Studios, off Goodge Street, over three intensive weekend sessions in February 1977. The record, whose 14 songs included 'White Riot' and 'London's Burning', was subsequently lauded as one of the greatest punk albums ever made. The Whitfield Street studios dealt with a wide variety of music during its time. Jimi Hendrix had recorded at CBS in 1966, and just months after the Clash were here, Bing Crosby popped in to record an album shortly before his death, cutting numbers like 'April Showers' and 'June Is Bustin' Out All Over'.

# OASIS
**34 Berwick Street, W1**

The photograph on the cover of Oasis' second album, *(What's the Story) Morning Glory?*, was taken here in the early hours of 27 July, 1995, and features an interesting trio: the London DJ Sean Rowley (facing the camera); Brian Cannon, who designed the album cover (with his back to us); and, in the distance on the left-hand pavement, Owen Morris, who co-produced the record. Legend has it that Morris is seen clutching the album's master tape. The location is a homage to the recording medium itself:

this was part of London's 'vinyl triangle', where crate-diggers would spend hours hunting for rare grooves (the much-missed emporium Selectadisc can be seen on the left). The two men in the photograph were originally meant to be Liam and Noel Gallagher, but they were apparently indisposed after a heavy night.

## MUMFORD & SONS
### 596 King's Road, SW6

To create the cover of their 2009 debut album, *Sigh No More*, the multimillion-selling folk-rock band stood in a shop window in this famous Chelsea thoroughfare, holding their instruments. The shop was Pimpernel & Partners, which sold elegant French furniture. Pimpernel has since moved on.

# NORTH LONDON

## LONNIE DONEGAN

Decca Studios,
165 Broadhurst Gardens,
NW6

On 13 July, 1954, Chris Barber's Jazz Band were recording the jazz album *New Orleans Joys* at Decca Studios in West Hampstead, when the banjo player Anthony 'Lonnie' Donegan casually added a spot of skiffle, as he usually did in their stage shows. He played four songs, including 'Rock Island Line', an old bluesy American folk tune about an Illinois railroad. Released as a single in 1955, the song went on to become a sensation, making a star of Lonnie Donegan and kicking off a craze for skiffle. Women across Britain began to wonder where their washboards had gone, and a generation of aspiring guitarists – including the young John Lennon, Paul McCartney and George Harrison – became keen skifflers. The record company was as surprised as everyone else: it hadn't rated 'Rock Island Line'. As Donegan recalled, 'Decca weren't at all keen. They thought folk music meant Cornish pasties and maypoles, with fa-la-la and a tooralay!'

## THE BEATLES

EMI Studios,
3 Abbey Road, NW8

The ultimate temple to recorded music, Abbey Road Studios in St John's Wood began life as a Regency town house, and was converted for use as a studio for classical music in the 1930s. This was still known simply as EMI Studios when the Beatles first came here. It took them one day to record their debut album, *Please Please Me*, but later works such as *Sgt Pepper* took months. Most of the songs the band ever recorded were taped in Studio Two, though some orchestral parts required the larger Studio One. They honoured the EMI facility by naming the last album they recorded together *Abbey Road*, and to create the cover they summoned just enough effort to stroll across the zebra crossing outside. Millions of tourists have since followed in their footsteps, while many other artists (including solo Beatles) have opted to record in the studios.

# PINK FLOYD
EMI Studios,
3 Abbey Road, NW8

The Floyd came here in 1967 to tape their debut album, *The Piper at the Gates of Dawn*, after which it became their favoured domain for recording. Their 1973 masterpiece *The Dark Side of the Moon* was fashioned here, before they wasted many expensive hours tinkering with non-musical instruments such as saucepans and elastic bands for their unfinished *Household Objects* project. By 1975 they had come to their senses, returned to their usual instruments and started recording the *Wish You Were Here* album. Spookily, while they were mixing 'Shine on You Crazy Diamond', their moving homage to former frontman Syd Barrett, they spotted a mysterious portly figure lurking in the studio. It was Syd.

# ROD STEWART
Morgan Studios,
169-171 High Road,
Willesden, NW10

The sandpaper-throated singer mingled rock, blues, soul and folk to create his 1971 album *Every Picture Tells a Story* at Morgan Studios, on the corner of Willesden High Road and Maybury Gardens. Widely considered the finest moment of Stewart's solo career (although the other members of the Faces played on it), the record topped the charts in the UK and the US, and yielded a chart-topping classic in 'Maggie May'. Earlier in the 20th century, the hulking Morgan Studios building had been used to make parts for aircraft.

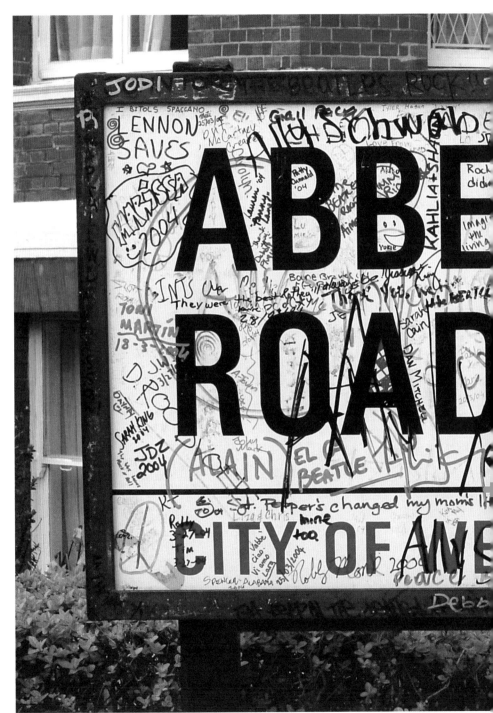

Local graffiti still celebrates the Beatles' recording career in St John's Wood.
*Photograph Misterweiss*

"TALES FROM TOPOGRAPHIC OCEANS IS LIKE A WOMAN'S PADDED BRA. THE COVER LOOKS GOOD, BUT WHEN YOU PEEL OFF THE PADDING, THERE'S NOT A LOT THERE."

RICK WAKEMAN

## YES

Morgan Studios,
169-171 High Road,
Willesden, NW10

Before they embarked on their epic 1973 album *Tales from Topographic Oceans* – a double album with just four side-long tracks – the members of Yes talked about whether they should record it in the city or somewhere leafier. Singer Jon Anderson fancied doing it in a tent pitched in a beautiful wood. They ultimately compromised, choosing Morgan Studios in London but bringing in some props to add a rural atmosphere, including bales of hay, a picket fence and a cow made out of cardboard. Keyboardist Rick Wakeman found much of the music tedious and relieved the boredom by playing keyboards on a track for Black Sabbath, who were simultaneously recording the album *Sabbath Bloody Sabbath* in an adjacent studio at Morgan. Sabbath's lead singer Ozzy Osbourne recalled giving Yes a lump of especially strong hashish, and then visiting their studio to find they'd gone home around midday after feeling unwell.

## THE SEX PISTOLS

Wessex Sound Studios,
106A Highbury New Park, N5

The Pistols skulked into Wessex Sound Studios in leafy Highbury in October 1976 to begin work on their only studio album. During the sporadic recording process, which dragged on through the spring and summer of 1977, the band were signed by A&M Records, then dropped, then signed by Virgin. The album, featuring 'God Save the Queen', 'Anarchy in the U.K.' and 'Pretty Vacant', was released in October as *Never Mind the Bollocks, Here's the Sex Pistols*. Virgin record shops were raided by police when they filled their windows with copies of the cover, and a legal argument ensued about the import of the B-word. Meanwhile the album shot to No. 1. The studio building had begun life as a Victorian gothic church hall, and in the 1940s housed the 'charm school' for the Rank Organisation, grooming British actors including Christopher Lee and Diana Dors for stardom.

## EURYTHMICS
**The Church Studios,**
**145H Crouch Hill, N8**

Annie Lennox and Dave Stewart converted this Victorian chapel building in Crouch End into a studio in the early 1980s, naming it the Church in honour of its former use. Part of their 1982 album *Sweet Dreams (Are Made of This)* came together here, and its follow-up *Touch* (including the songs 'Here Comes the Rain Again' and 'Who's That Girl') was recorded here in the summer of 1983. In 1996, Alisha's Attic chose the Church for the creation of their feisty debut album, *Alisha Rules the World* (produced by Stewart), and other Church-goers have included Bob Dylan, Elvis Costello and Radiohead. In 2004 the singer David Gray acquired the building, and in 2013 it was acquired by the producer and Adele collaborator Paul Epworth.

## THE POGUES & KIRSTY MacCOLL
**RAK Studios,**
**42-48 Charlbert Street, NW8**

In 1987 the Pogues laboured on their third album, *If I Should Fall from Grace with God*, at RAK Studios, established by producer Mickie Most in a Victorian school and church hall in St John's Wood. During the sessions they fished out a song they had been playing with, unsuccessfully, over the past two years – a duet about a couple bickering in New York City over the Christmas period. The band's producer, Steve Lillywhite, took the recording back to his home studio and asked his wife, Kirsty MacColl, to sing the female lines. The results impressed the Pogues, and singer Shane MacGowan completed his vocal parts separately at RAK. 'Fairytale of New York', composed by MacGowan and Jem Finer and named after JP Donleavy's 1973 novel, became an all-time classic – the most-played Christmas song of the 21st century, with double-platinum sales and regular prizes for 'best-ever festive tune'.

# THE STREETS
## Kestrel House, City Road, N1

Original Pirate Material, the 2002 debut album by the Streets (alias rapper Mike Skinner), features an atmospheric night-time scene on its cover. It shows Kestrel House, an 18-storey block of flats in Islington. The photograph, entitled Towering Inferno, was taken in 1995 using a long exposure by the German photographer and artist Rut Blees Luxemburg, and chimes well with the gritty urban realism of Skinner's lyrics.

# WEST LONDON

## THE SMALL FACES
**Olympic Sound Studios,
117-123 Church Road, SW13**

The Small Faces recorded most of their 'cockneydelic' classic *Ogdens' Nut Gone Flake* at Olympic Sound Studios in Barnes from late 1967 to the spring of 1968. Side two of this early concept album relates the tale of Happiness Stan and his quest for the missing half of the moon, and includes 'loonie links' from the master of comedy nonsense, Stanley Unwin (Spike Milligan was asked, but declined to take part). The Rolling Stones had spent much of 1967 at Olympic Sound recording their own psychedelic album, *Their Satanic Majesties Request*, and Procol Harum also cut their classic 'A Whiter Shade of Pale' here. The Olympic building had enjoyed a colourful history before bands came to record in Barnes. In the early 20th century it was a combined cinema and theatre, in which actors such as John Gielgud and Charles Laughton trod the boards.

## CARLY SIMON
**Portobello Hotel,
22 Stanley Gardens, W11**

The American singer-songwriter posed for a series of photographs at Trident Studios while she recorded her 1972 album *No Secrets*, featuring the classic put-down song 'You're So Vain'. But the photographer, Ed Caraeff, wasn't sure he had nailed the right shot for the cover, so he carried on snapping as Simon left Soho and returned to

Ed Caraeff's photographs of Carly Simon in front of the Portobello Hotel were used to promote her debut album in 1972. © *Ed Caraeff/Morgan Media Partners*

the chic Portobello Hotel in Notting Hill. The favoured image shows the behatted star in a casual stance, bag slung over her shoulder, in front of the fancy iron railings of the hotel.

## BOB MARLEY & THE WAILERS
**Island Records,
8-10 Basing Street, W11**

Following an attempt on his life in his Jamaican homeland, Bob Marley settled in London in 1977, and he and the Wailers spent several weeks in Island Records' Notting Hill studios, on the corner of Basing Street and Lancaster Road. The sessions yielded the acclaimed album *Exodus* (including the singles 'Exodus', 'Jamming', 'Waiting in Vain' and 'Three Little Birds'), as well as its smoother and happier follow-up, *Kaya* (featuring 'Is This Love?', 'Sun Is Shining' and 'Satisfy My Soul').

## BAND AID
**Sarm West Studio,
8-10 Basing Street, W11**

On Sunday, 25 November, 1984, when the cream of 1980s pop answered the call to record a charity single for the starving people of Ethiopia, the producer Trevor Horn donated the use of his studio Sarm West, formerly known as Basing Street Studios. Phil Collins recalled: 'I was finishing my album *No Jacket Required* at the Townhouse in London, and one night I got a call from Bob Geldof, asking if I'd seen the news about Ethiopia. I said I hadn't, because I'd been working, and he said he wanted to do something about it, and he wanted a famous drummer.' Collins pitched up at the studio, where other attendees included Boy George, Bono, George Michael, Paul Weller, Paul Young and Bananarama, and the whole company recorded the Bob Geldof/Midge Ure song 'Do They Know It's Christmas?', with its rousing chorus of 'Feed the world'. The record sold millions, and successive Band Aid singles were recorded in other studios in 1989, 2004 and 2014.

# MUMFORD & SONS

**Eastcote Studios,
249 Kensal Road, W10**

The west London folk-rock quartet recorded their debut album, *Sigh No More*, between 2008 and 2009 at Eastcote Studios. The recording facility is confusingly a long way from Eastcote in northwest London, being situated in Kensal Town, north of Notting Hill. The album made precise categorisation tricky, combining folk and rock with country and bluegrass influences and quotations from Shakespeare; one review said it was 'basically an indie-pop record in chunky-knit clothing'. *Rolling Stone* magazine opined: 'If Dexys Midnight Runners aged into boozy pub-session romantics, they might sound like Mumford and Sons'. Although reviews were mixed, the record won a Brit Award for Best Album and gradually picked up a large crowd of supporters, selling a million copies in the UK, hitting No. 2 in the British chart, and shifting three million copies in the US. Mumford & Sons returned here to record their 2012 follow-up album, *Babel*. Adele's 2010 song 'Rolling in the Deep', her first American No. 1, was recorded in the same studios.

# EAST
# LONDON

## QUEEN

**Sarm East Studios,
9-13 Osborn Street, E1**

Freddie Mercury and his colleagues recorded large chunks of their 1975 album *A Night at the Opera* at Sarm East Studios, on this site between Brick Lane and Whitechapel High Street. Tracks cut here included 'Lazing on a Sunday Afternoon', 'I'm in Love with My Car', 'Seaside Rendezvous', 'The Prophet's Song' and even parts of 'Bohemian Rhapsody', which was evidently too monstrous to be confined to one studio. Queen would return to Osborn Street to work on tracks for their subsequent two albums, *A Day at the Races* and *News of the World*.

## ENYA

**Orinoco Studios,
36 Leroy Street, SE1**

The Irish singer scored an unexpected hit with her second album, *Watermark*, which was finished here at Orinoco Studios, off the Old Kent Road, in 1988. The ethereal neo-Celtic tracks included the chart-topping single 'Orinoco Flow (Sail Away)', which took part of its title from the name of the studios (which had borrowed it from the famous river in South America).

# THE WHITE STRIPES
**Toe Rag Studios,
166A Glyn Road, E5**

'No computers were used during the writing, recording, mixing, or mastering of this record,' proclaimed the White Stripes on their 2003 release *Elephant*. Jack and Meg White went back to basics with the album, recording most of it over ten days in Toe Rag Studios on the edge of Hackney Marsh. Toe Rag, established by British producer Liam Watson, quickly became renowned for using vintage analogue equipment, as well as an old mixing console from Abbey Road Studios and a 1965 Ludwig drum kit. The White Stripes recorded using the studio's old-style stc 4021 'ball and biscuit' microphones, which apparently inspired one of the tracks, 'Ball and Biscuit'. *Rolling Stone* magazine declared the experiment a great success, calling the album 'a work of pulverizing perfection'. Explaining their choice of studio, Jack White said: 'You could find the same equipment in America, but they also have all this computer digital equipment, which I hate. When it's not even there, no engineer will try and talk you into it. It's not trying to sound retro – it's just recognising what was the pinnacle of recording technology... Some bands spend millions of dollars, rent a studio in LA and have, like, video games to play between takes. I think a cup of tea was probably our only entertainment.'

# RUDIMENTAL
**15 Dalston Lane, E8**

The cover of *Home*, the 2013 debut album by the East London drum-and-bass outfit Rudimental, shows the Hackney Peace Carnival Mural. This huge and vibrant artwork near the junction with Kingsland High Street was painted by the artist Ray Walker in the 1980s, and depicts the Hackney Peace Carnival of 1983, in which local activists marched in support of nuclear disarmament. The much-loved mural had degraded and been obscured by fencing over the years, but was restored to its former glory in 2014. It can now be seen opposite Dalston Junction station on the Overground.

# SOUTH LONDON

## DEPECHE MODE

**Blackwing Studios,
All Hallows Church,
Copperfield Street, SE1**

The Essex electronic combo came to Borough to record their 1981 debut album, *Speak & Spell*, at Blackwing Studios in this Victorian church, which had been wrecked by bombs during the Blitz. After founder member and songwriter Vince Clarke left the band to form Yazoo, they auditioned candidates for his replacement in this studio, hiring Alan Wilder. Their second album, *A Broken Frame*, was also recorded at Blackwing, though singer Dave Gahan admitted to being unsettled by the location. 'It's a really strange place. There's a statue of Christ on the cross that someone's painted with blood outside in the garden,' he told an interviewer. 'We had a load of photos [taken] down there, but none of those came out. It's really weird.' Yazoo also recorded here, as did the Cocteau Twins and Stereolab, before the studios closed down in 2001.

## PINK FLOYD

**Battersea Power Station, SW8**

In the days before everybody's grandmother had mastered Photoshop, the Floyd's artwork supremo Storm Thorgerson decreed that a giant inflatable pig, 30 feet long and 20 feet high, should be flown above London's most famous power station to illustrate the band's 1977 album *Animals*. What could possibly go wrong? High winds caused the porker to tear loose from its tether. It drifted into the airspace

Pink Floyd's 30-foot-long inflatable pig flying high over Battersea Power Station.
*Keystone/Hulton Archive/Getty Images*

used by passenger flights, and finished its aerial journey with a bumpy landing in a farmer's field in Kent. The story generated a suspiciously useful welter of free publicity for the new album.

# KYLIE MINOGUE
**PWL Studios,**
**4-7 The Vineyard,**
**Sanctuary Street, SE1**

It was at PWL Studios that Stock, Aitken and Waterman (SAW) transformed mainstream pop music in the 1980s, harnessing the energy of club music to propel highly infectious songs into the charts. PWL (Pete Waterman Limited) Studios, behind Borough Tube station, became known as 'the Hit Factory' as a result. Kylie Minogue was an actress in the Australian soap *Neighbours* when she came to these studios in 1987, apparently with an appointment to see the producer Pete Waterman. Waterman had forgotten and wasn't here – he was back home in Merseyside, which was unfortunate since Minogue was due to fly home later that day. His business partner Mike Stock called him to say Minogue was here and expecting to do some recording now, to which Waterman is said to have replied: 'She should be so lucky.' A song was hastily cobbled together by Stock and Waterman, and the Australian chanteuse was soon behind a microphone singing 'I Should Be So Lucky', which became a global smash. Other benefactors of the SAW sound include Rick Astley and Bananarama.

# STORMZY
**91a Peterborough Road, SW6**

The 2017 album by the grime star from Thornton Heath, *Gang Signs & Prayer,* was recorded at producer Fraser T. Smith's studio in the Matrix Complex, Parsons Green. Smith explained: 'In the making of the record, it was literally four people who had heard the album, which is really unusual. There were no people casually dropping in to hear it – no record companies, no anything. So when it reached the point where we did the final track listing and Stormzy and I

came to play it to people, it was absolutely nerve-racking.'
The risk paid off: the album became the first grime album to
top the UK album charts. It was also critically well received,
one reviewer calling it 'a multi-faceted masterpiece and a
testament to Stormzy's talent that warrants his phenomenal
rise to the top'.

ISBN: 9 781 78884 016 3

First published by ACC Art Books in 2019
Reprinted 2023

British Library Cataloguing-in-Publication Data
A catalogue record for this book is available from the British
Library

The author and publisher gratefully acknowledge the permission
granted to reproduce the copyright material in this book. Every
effort has been made to trace copyright holders and to obtain
their permission for the use of copyright material. The publisher
apologises for any errors or omissions in the text and would be
grateful if notified of any corrections that should be incorporated
in future reprints or editions of this book.

Design concept: Webb & Webb Design Ltd.

Front cover: The Rolling Stones in Tin Pan Alley, photographed by
Terry O'Neill, 1963. © *Terry O'Neill/Iconic Images*

Frontispiece: The Who in Piccadilly Circus, June 1964. The
photograph was taken during a brief period in which the
band were performing under the name The High Numbers.
*Tracksimages.com/Alamy Stock Photo*

Pages 4-5: The Marquee Club during its famous residency on
Wardour Street, Soho, 1970s.
*Ray Stevenson/REX/Shutterstock*

MIX
Paper from
responsible sources
FSC® C124385

Printed in China
for ACC Art Books Ltd., Woodbridge, Suffolk, UK

www.accartbooks.com

ACC
ART
BOOKS